I0309353

Drift

A Collection Curated by Eden Cottage Yarns

Eden Cottage Yarns 2017

Third edition
June 2017

First published September 2015

Copyright
Eden Cottage Yarns Ltd

All rights reserved

No part of this book may be reproduced or transmitted in any form or by any means, electronic, mechanical, photocopying, recording or otherwise, without prior permission from the publisher. The complimentary digital version of this book must not be resold or distributed separately from the printed book.

Photography: Victoria Magnus and David O'Kelly
Honey Bee Photography: Kay Bingham

Technical Editing: Clare Devine
Technical Editing of Beulah: Jo Kelly
Technical Editing of Turbine: Eleanor Dixon
Crochet Technical Editing: Alison Casserley
Copy Editing: Jo Milmine

(special thanks to David O'Kelly and Liam Devine for proof reading)

Layout: Clare Devine

Published by: Eden Cottage Yarns Ltd

Printed in the UK

- 978-0-9931618-2-7

Eden Cottage Yarns

Contents

Introduction	2
The Collection	5
Patterns	
Cloudburst by Dieuwke van Mulligen	42
Pimms Cup by Thea Colman	49
Hardcastle by Louise Tilbrook	52
Deco Swirl by Louise Zass-Bangham	54
Ja Ja by Åsa Tricosa	56
Beulah by Clare Devine	68
Embleton by Tracey Todhunter	72
Swale by Karie Westermann	74
Bothel by Tracey Todhunter	76
Turbine by Justyna Lorkowska	78
Caldbeck by Tracey Todhunter	84
Honey Bee by Dani Sunshine	86
Abbreviations	92
On Location	95
About the Designers	115
About the Yarn	121

Welcome to the second Eden Cottage Yarns collection.

This carefully curated collection drifts through the seasons; each beautiful design draws elements from the designer's personal style and showcases our sumptuous Whitfell DK range. We wanted to create space for each designer to stamp their own personality within the collection, with us functioning as curators, or the chief enablers.

We hope you fall in love with this collection as much as we have. Comprising of a wonderful selection of garments and accessories, this collection features ten beautiful designs; each piece has a touch of Eden Cottage Yarns woodland-inspired whimsy. There are garments for women and children and a beautiful mix of accessories, including items for crochet and knitting.

Each piece has been carefully crafted to add a touch of warmth to your wardrobe, whatever the season. Whitfell DK is incredibly versatile, as shown in this glorious collection of designs. It can be used to make light fabrics with exquisite drape, perfect for warding off the chill on a cool summer evening, or worked to a dense and cosy fabric ideal for the depths of winter.

The collection has been photographed in our beloved Yorkshire. We hope you enjoy the glimpses behind the scenes and the majestic landscape of the county we call home.

Victoria and David.

The Collection

Cloudburst
by Dieuwke van Mulligen

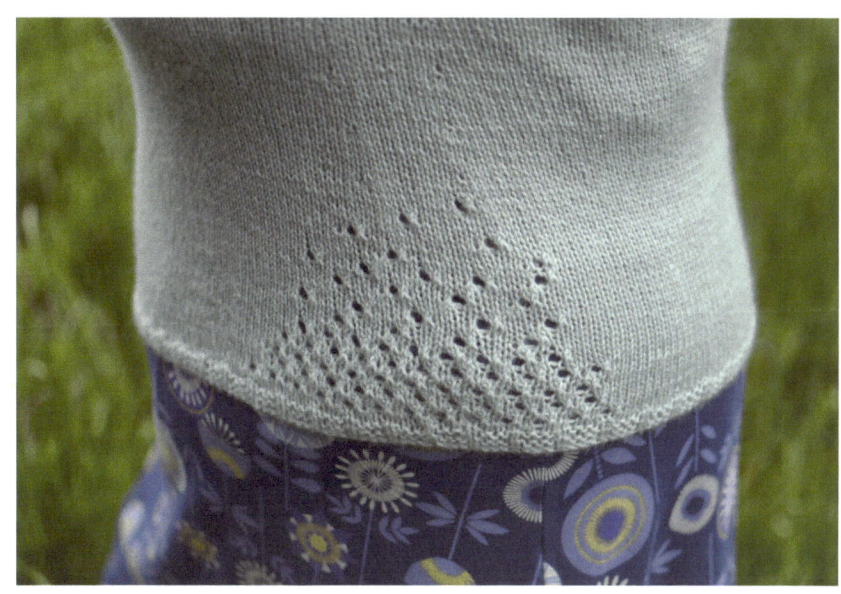

Pimms Cup by Thea Colman

Hardcastle by Louise Tilbrook

Deco Swirl by Louise Zass-Bangham

Ja Ja by Åsa Tricosa

Beulah by Clare Devine

Embleton by Tracey Todhunter

Swale by Karie Westermann

Bothel by
Tracey Todhunter

Turbine by Justyna Lorkowska

Caldbeck by Tracey Todhunter

Honey Bee by Dani Sunshine

The Patterns

Cloudburst
Dieuwke van Mulligen

You know that feeling you have when it gets colder, you just want to curl up next to the fire, hot cocoa in hand? This sweater is designed for just that occasion. Envelop yourself in the beautifully soft Whitfell DK and pull the generous long sleeves down over your hands for that cozy snuggle-up feeling. The eyelet details give the sweater subtle and interesting features, both to knit and wear. With this pattern on the needles, you'll already picture yourself sitting by the fire and sipping that hot cocoa. Available in nine sizes from XS to 5XL.

Materials

Eden Cottage Yarns Whitfell DK (DK; 100% baby Alpaca; 100m / 109yds per 50g ball)
Shade: Misty Woods; 8 (8, 9, 11, 12, 13, 14, 16, 17) x 50g balls

Needles and Accessories

3.5 mm (US 4) circular needle, 80cm / 32in length (or the size needed to obtain the correct gauge)
3.25 mm (US 3) circular needle, 60cm / 24in length, for working neckline
If desired, one set of 3.5 mm / US 4 DPNs for sleeves. You can also use the magic loop method

Four stitch markers, tapestry needle for weaving in ends

Sizes

XS (S, M, L, XL, 2XL, 3XL, 4XL, 5XL)
Finished circumference: 76 (86, 96, 106, 116, 124, 136, 146, 156)cm / 30 (33.75, 37.75, 41.75, 45.75, 48.75, 53.5, 57.5, 61.5)in
To fit: 74 84, 94, 104, 114, 124, 135, 145, 155)cm / 29 (33, 37, 41, 45, 49, 53, 57, 61)in

Please refer to detailed schematic at the end of this pattern for more sizing details.

Gauge

20 sts and 27 rounds to 10cm (4in) over stocking stitch, in the round, on 3.5 mm / US 4 needles after blocking.

Note: Adjust needle size if necessary to match gauge.

Pattern Notes

The sweater is worked top down with a raglan construction, incorporating an eyelet stitch pattern on the right shoulder only. The top of the yoke is worked flat and then joined in the round to form a rounded neckline. When the yoke reaches the desired length, stitches are set aside for sleeves. The body is worked in the round, adding some slight waist shaping. Another eyelet detail is done on the bottom left side of the body.
Sleeves are worked top down. Stitches are then picked up along the neckline to give it a neat finishing.

Pattern

Using larger needles, cast on 78 (80, 82, 86, 86, 86, 88, 96) sts.

PM as follows (WS):
P3 (right front), pm, p17 (17, 17, 17, 17, 17, 17, 17, 21) (right shoulder), pm, p38 (40, 42, 46, 46, 46, 46, 48, 48) (back), pm, p17 (17, 17, 17, 17, 17, 17, 17, 21) (left shoulder), pm, p3 (left front).

Set up row 1 (RS): *K1, m1l, k to 1 st before m, M1R, k1, sm,* repeat *-* 4 times more. 10 sts increased
Set up row 2 (WS): Purl, slipping markers.

Work single incs for front neckline:
Row 1: *K1, m1l, k to 1 st before m, M1R, k1, sm,* (left front) repeat *-* twice (left shoulder, back), work Sleeve Detail Chart 1 row 1 (right shoulder), sm, repeat *-* once more. 10 sts increased
Row 2: Purl, slipping markers.

Rpt last 2 rows 2 (3, 2, 4, 4, 4, 4, 3, 3) more times, working subsequent chart rows over the right shoulder sts. Note that the eyelet pattern is on every 3 rows, thus happens on a WS row every second time.

Total sts 118 (130, 122, 146, 146, 146, 146, 138, 146)
Stitch count divided as follows:
Fronts are each: 11 (13, 11, 15, 15, 15, 15, 13, 13) sts
Back is: 46 (50, 50, 58, 58, 58, 58, 58, 58) sts
Sleeves are each: 25 (27, 25, 29, 29, 29, 29, 27, 31) sts
You are ending with a chart row: 6 (8, 6, 10, 10, 10, 10, 8, 8)

Work double incs for front neckline:
Double inc row 1 (RS): *K1, M1L, k to 1 st before m, M1R, k1, sm,* repeat *-* twice, work chart, sm, repeat *-* once more. 10 sts increased.
Double inc row 2 (WS): P1, M1L, p to 1 st before end, M1R, p1. 2 sts increased.

Rpt last 2 double inc rows, 2 (2, 3, 3, 3, 3, 3, 4, 4) more times.
Total sts 154 (166, 170, 194, 194, 194, 194, 198, 206)

Stitch count divided as follows:
Fronts are each: 20 (22, 23, 27, 27, 27, 27, 28, 28) sts
Back is: 52 (56, 58, 66, 66, 66, 66, 68, 68) sts
Sleeves are each: 31 (33, 33, 37, 37, 37, 37, 37, 41) sts
You are ending with a chart row: 12 (14, 14, 18, 18, 18, 18, 18, 18)

Join fronts:
Joining rnd (RS): K to 1 st before m, M1R, k1, sm, *k1, M1L, k to 1 st before m, M1R, k1, sm,* repeat *-* once, work chart, sm, M1L, k to end, backwards loop CO 12 sts, join in the round, k to m.
20 sts increased (8 for raglan, 12 for CO)

Beginning of round is now at the left front of raglan. You have ended with a 13 (15, 15, 19, 19, 19, 19, 19, 19) of the Sleeve Detail Chart 1.
Stitch count:
Front is: 54 (58, 60, 68, 68, 68, 68, 70, 70) sts
Back is: 54 (58, 60, 68, 68, 68, 68, 70, 70) sts
Sleeves are each: 33 (35, 35, 39, 39, 39, 39, 39, 43) sts

Work sleeve and raglan incs:
Rnd 1: (K to m, sm) twice, work Sleeve Detail Chart 2 starting at Rnd 1 (3, 3, 7, 7, 7, 7, 7, 7), sm, k to m.
Rnd 2: (K1, M1L, k to 1 st before m, M1R, k1, sm) twice, work chart, sm, M1L, k to 1 st before end, M1R, k1. 8 sts increased.
Rpt last rnds 6 (4, 6, 5, 6, 9, 9, 11, 6) times more.

Note that for sizes XS-XL you will end on chart row: 14 (12, 16, 18, 22); for size 5XL you will end on chart row 20.

For sizes 2XL-4XL you will end the chart before you have finished all inc rnds. Here, insert an increase on the right hand sleeve on either side just like on the left sleeve.
Total sts 230 (226, 246, 262, 270, 294, 294, 312, 280)

43

Stitch count:
Front is: 68 (68, 74, 80, 82, 88, 88, 94, 84) sts
Back is: 68 (68, 74, 80, 82, 88, 88, 94, 84) sts
Sleeves are each: 47 (45, 49, 51, 53, 59, 59, 63, 57) sts

Work raglan incs only:
Sizes XS-XL:
Rnd 1: (K to m, sm) twice, work Sleeve Detail Chart 3 starting at Rnd 3 (1, 5, 7, 11), sm, k to m.

Sizes 2XL-4XL:
Rnd 1: Knit, slipping markers.

Size 5XL:
Rnd 1: (K to m, sm) twice, work Sleeve Detail Chart 3 starting at Rnd 9, sm, k to m.

All sizes:
Rnd 2: *K to m, sm, k1, M1L, k to 1 st before m, M1R, sm*, repeat *-* once more. 4 sts increased
Rpt last 2 rnds 0(3, 5, 6, 7, 6, 8, 8, 13) more times.

Stitch count:
Front is: 70 (76, 86, 94, 98, 102, 106, 112, 112) sts
Back is: 70 (76, 86, 94, 98, 102, 106, 112, 112) sts
Sleeves are each: 47 (45, 49, 51, 53, 59, 59, 63, 57) sts

Work straight without increases until armhole depth measures approximately 19 (20, 22, 23, 24, 25, 27, 28, 29)cm / 7.5 (7.75, 8.75, 9, 9.5, 9.75, 10.75, 11, 11.5)in.

Divide for sleeves:
RM, put sleeve sts on hold, CO 3 (5, 5, 6, 9, 11, 15, 17, 22) sts, pm (left side marker and beginning of rnd), CO 3 (5, 5, 6, 9, 11, 15, 17, 22) sts, rm, k to m, rm, put sleeve sts on hold, CO 3 (5, 5, 6, 9, 11, 15, 17, 22) sts, pm (right side marker), CO 3 (5, 5, 6, 9, 11, 15, 17, 22) sts, rm, k to end.
Body is: 152 (172, 192, 212, 232, 248, 272, 292, 312) sts

Work body in stocking stitch (k every rnd) until you reach 5cm / 2in from dividing for sleeves, then work dec rnd:
K5, ssk, k until 7 sts before m, k2tog, k to m, sm, repeat *-* once. 4 sts decreased

Work dec rnd every 3cm / 1.25in (approx. every 8th rnd) a total of 3 times.
Body sts are: 140 (160, 180, 200, 220, 236, 260, 280, 300) sts

Work 5cm straight, then work inc rnd:
K5, m1l, k until 5 sts before m, M1R, k to m, sm, repeat *-* once. 4 sts increased

Work inc rnd every 3 cm / 1.25 inches (appr every 8th rnd) a total of 4 times.

After inc rnds are done, body sts are: 156 (176, 196, 216, 236, 252, 276, 296, 316) sts

Work straight until body measures 36 (37, 38, 39, 40, 41, 42, 43, 44)cm / 14.25 (14.5, 15, 15.25, 15.75, 16.25, 16.5, 17, 17.25)in, measured from underarm.

AT THE SAME TIME:
When body measures approximately 21.5 (22.5, 23.5, 24.5, 25.5, 26.5, 27.5, 28.5, 29.5)cm / 8.5 (8.75, 9.25, 9.75, 10, 10.5, 10.75, 11.25, 11.5)in, start working body detail chart on left side of the body.
Start working chart row 1 from 21 sts before left side marker/beginning of rnd; the yellow cells on the chart indicate the placement of the marker.
Note: If you want to lengthen the body, work more straight rnds before starting body detail chart.

Work bottom hem:
Rnd 1: *K1, p3; rpt from * around.
Rnd 2: Knit.

Rpt last 2 rnds once, then rnd 1 once more. Cast off knitwise.

Sleeves:
Starting at the middle of the CO sts, pick up and knit 3 (5, 5, 6, 9, 11, 15, 17, 22) sts, k sleeve sts, pick up and knit 3 (5, 5, 6, 9, 11, 15, 17, 22) sts in remaining CO sts, pm for beginning of rnd. 53 (55, 59, 63, 71, 81, 89, 97, 101) sts

Work straight in stocking stitch until sleeve measures 25cm / 5in from underarm, then start decreasing:
Dec rnd: K1, k2tog, k until 3 sts before end, ssk, k1. 2 sts decreased

Work the dec rnd every 8 rows 5 more times. 41 (43, 47, 51, 59, 69, 77, 85, 89) sts

Work straight until sleeve measures 44 (45, 45, 46.5, 46.5, 47.5, 47.5, 49, 49)cm / 17.25 (17.75, 17.75, 18.25, 18.25, 18.75, 18.75, 19.25, 19.25)in, then work cuff:

Sizes XS-2XL-3XL-4XL-5XL:
Rnd 1: K2tog, p3, *k1, p3; rpt from * to end of rnd.

Sizes S-M-L-XL:
Rnd 1: Kfb, p2, *k1, p3; rpt from * to end of rnd.

All sizes:
Rnd 2: Knit.
Rnd 3: *K1, p3; rpt from * to end of rnd.
Rnd 4: Knit.
Rnd 5: *K1, p3; rpt from * to end of rnd.

Cast off knitwise.

Neckline finishing:
With smaller needles, pick up sts along the neckline; pick up one st for every horizontal st, and approximately 2 sts for every 3 rows. Make sure the number of sts you pick up is divisible by 4.
Row 1: *K1, p3; rpt from * to end of rnd.
Row 2: Knit.
Repeat last 2 rnds once, then rnd 1 once more. Cast off knitwise.

Finishing:
Weave in ends and wet block to size, making sure not to stretch the fabric too much. Alpaca is prone to stretching when wet if not treated gently .

Schematic

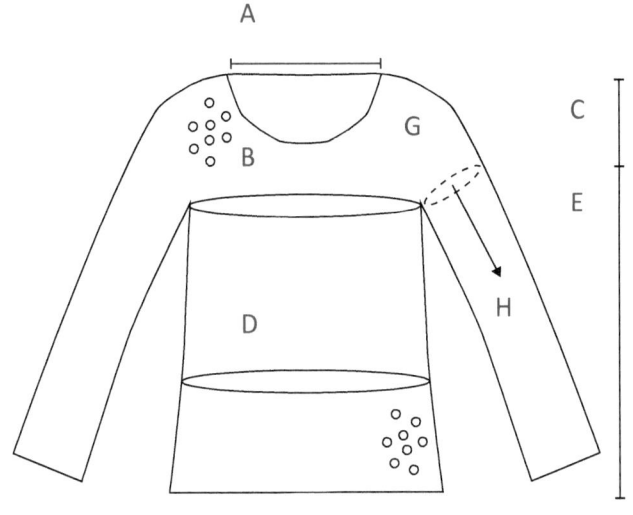

A) Back neck: 19 (20, 21, 23, 23, 23, 23, 24, 24)cm / 7.5 (8, 8.25, 9, 9, 9, 9, 9.5, 9.5)in

B) Bust: 76 (86, 96, 106, 116, 124, 136, 146, 156)cm / 30 (33.75, 37.75, 41.75, 45.75, 48.75, 53.5, 57.5, 61.5)in

C) Armhole depth: 19 (20, 22, 23, 24, 25, 27, 28, 29)cm / 7.5 (7.75, 8.75, 9, 9.5, 9.75, 10.75, 11, 11.5)in

D) Waist: 140 (160, 180, 200, 220, 236, 260, 280, 300)cm / 27.5 (31.5, 35.5, 39.5, 43.5, 46.5, 51.25, 55.25, 59)in

E) Length from underarm: 36 (37, 38, 39, 40, 41, 42, 43, 44)cm / 14.25 (14.5, 15, 15.25, 15.75, 16.25, 16.5, 17, 17.25)in

F) Total length: 55 (57, 60, 62, 64, 66, 69, 71, 73)cm / 21.75 (22.25, 23.75, 24.25, 25.25, 26, 27.25, 28, 18.75)in

G) Sleeve circumference: 26.5 (27.5, 29.5, 31.5, 35.5, 40.5, 44.5, 48.5, 50.5)cm / 10.5 (11, 11.75, 12.5, 14, 16, 17.5, 19, 20)in

H) Sleeve length from underarm: 44 (45, 45, 46.5, 46.5, 47.5, 47.5, 49, 49)cm /17.25 (17.75, 17.75, 18.25, 18.25, 18.75, 18.75, 19.25, 19.25)in

Chart

Sleeve Detail Chart 1

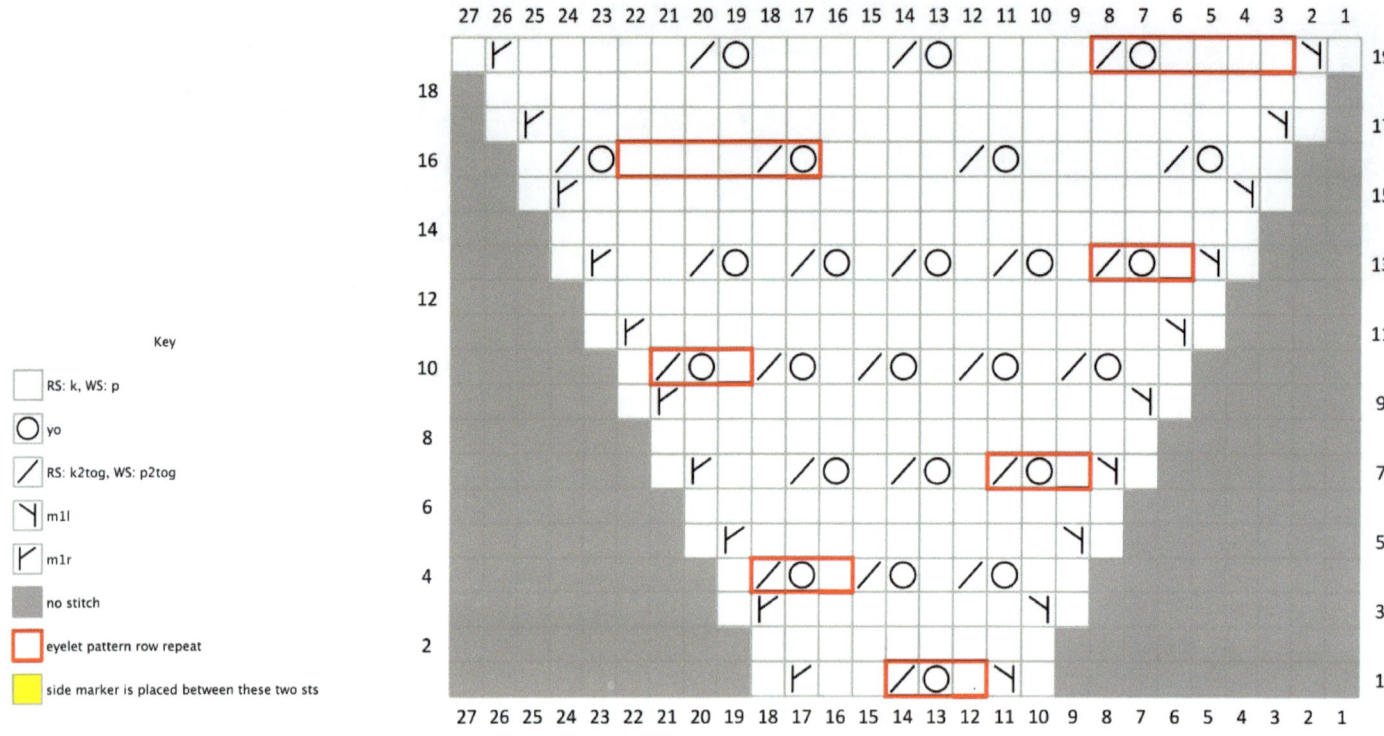

Sleeve Detail Chart 2

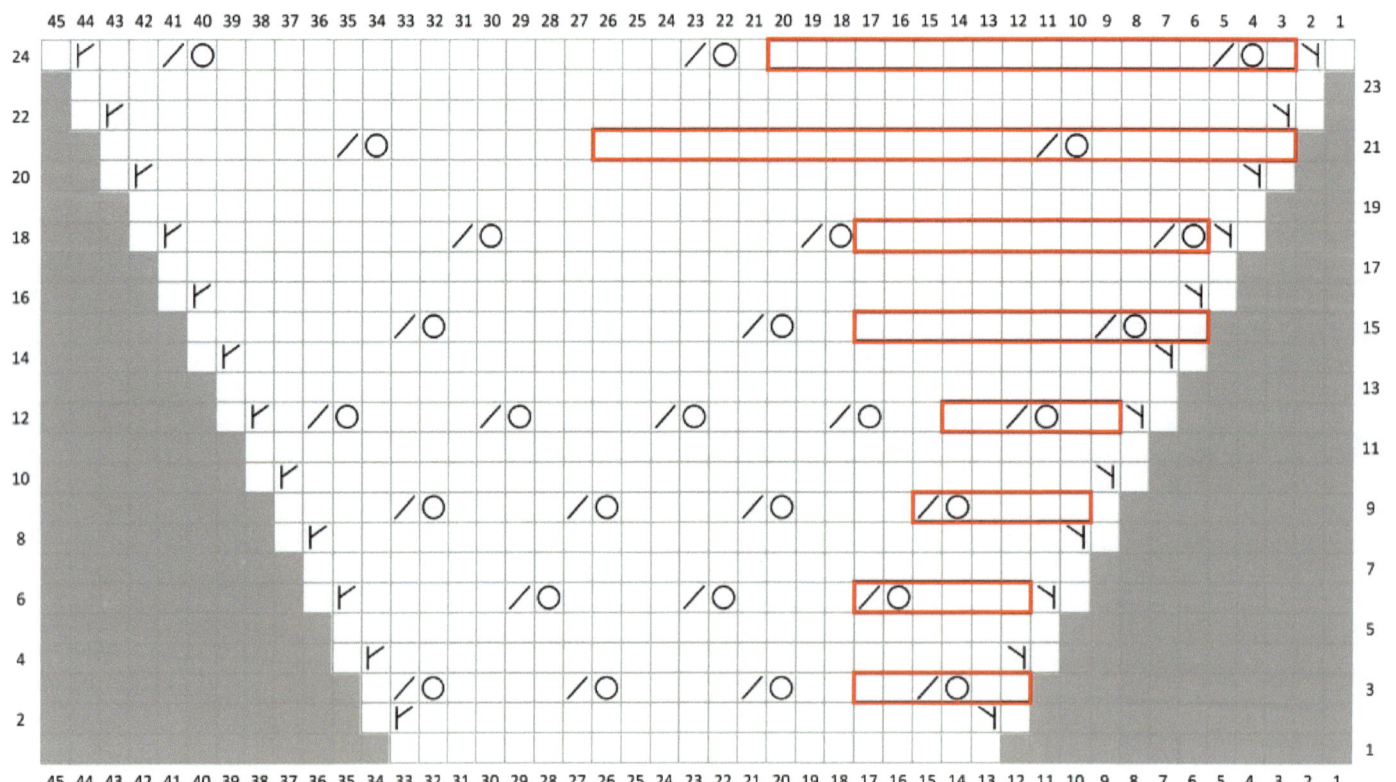

Sleeve Detail Chart 3

Body Eyelet Chart

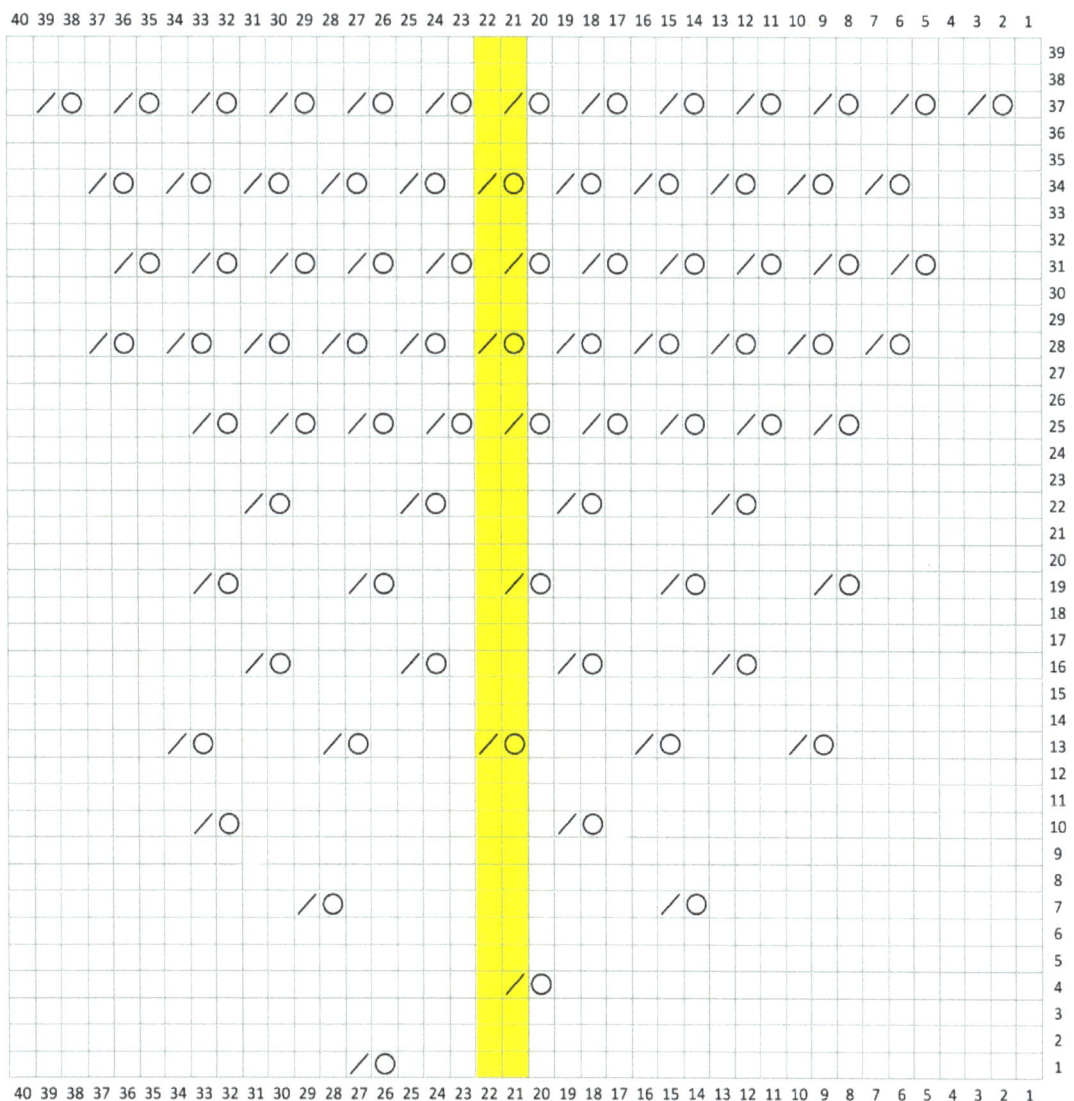

47

Pimms Cup
Thea Colman

This soft, slouchy hat features a deep ribbing that flows effortlessly into an alternating lace leaves and twisted cables pattern, giving the hat a lovely balance of textures whilst being fun to knit. It's the perfect accompaniment to kicking through crunchy autumn leaves before heading to a cosy country pub. Add a bobble to the top to bring a fun element to this piece.

Materials

Eden Cottage Yarns Whitfell DK (DK, 100% baby Alpaca; 100m / 109yds per 50g ball)
Shade: Dogwood; 2 x 50g ball(s)

Needles and Accessories

3.25mm (US 3) circular needles, 30 - 40cm (12-16in) length (or the size needed to obtain the correct gauge)
3.75mm (US 5) circular needles, 30 - 40cm (12-16in) length (or the size needed to obtain the correct gauge)
One set of DPNs in larger size for crown.

Note: If you would like hat to be a bit smaller or larger, go up or down one needle size.

Stitch marker, darning needle

Sizes

One size
Finished brim circumference: 42.5cm /16.75in
Finished hat circumference: 45.75cm /18 in
To fit: 50.75cm / 20in

Length: 24cm / 9.5in

Note: sizing may seem small, however the Alpaca yarn creates a knitted fabric that will stretch to fit.

Gauge

28 sts and 32 rounds to 10cm (4in) over ribbing stitch, in the round, on 3.25mm/US 3 needles after blocking.

26 sts and 30 rounds to 10 cm (4in) over lace and cable stitch, in the round, on 3.75mm/US 5 needles after blocking.

Note: Adjust needle size if necessary to match gauge.

Pattern Notes

If you would like to modify the hat for a shorter, more fitted shape, work one less repeat of the main lace motif. In order to adjust width, I suggest changing needle size as discussed in the materials section. Stitch counts within the pattern are not easily altered.

Pattern

Cast on 119 sts and join to work in the round, being careful not to twist sts. Place marker to indicate beginning of rnd.

Setup/Ribbing:
Rnd 1 (RS): *K1, p2, k1, p2, (k1, p1) 4 times, k1, p2; rep from * to end.

Work Rnd 1 for 20 rnds.

Transition to Lace:
Continue using your smaller needle for your first repeat of Rnds 1 and 2 of the chart. Switch to larger needle on Rnd 3 and continue with larger needle for rest of hat.

Chart Directions:

Work from chart for next 42 rnds to create main section of hat.

Chart is read bottom to top, right to left. Each row is a RS row.

Work chart rounds 1-14 three times. Work columns 1-17 seven times on each rnd.

Written Chart Directions (Main Section):
Chart rounds 1, 3, 5: *Work right twist, work left twist, p2, ssk, k2, yo, k1, yo, k2, k2tog, p2; rep from * to end.

All even numbered chart rnds 2-18: K4, p2, k9, p2

Chart rnd 7: *Work right twist, work left twist, p2, yo, k2tog, k5, ssk, yo, p2; rep from * to end.

Chart rnd 9: *Work right twist, work left twist, p2, k1, yo, k2tog, k3, ssk, yo, k1, p2; rep from * to end.

Chart rnd 11: *Work right twist, work left twist, p2, k2, yo, k2tog, k1, ssk, yo, k2, p2; rep from * to end.

Chart rnd 13: *Work right twist, work left twist, p2, k3, yo, sk2po, yo, k3, p2; rep from * to end.

Crown Section: Work chart rnds 15-28 once to complete hat. Work Columns 1-17 seven times on each round.

Written Chart Directions (Crown Section):
Chart rnds 15, 17, 19: *Work right twist, work left twist, p2, ssk, k2, yo, k1, yo, k2, k2tog, p2; rep from * to end.
Chart rnds 16, 19, 20: *K4, p2, k9, p2; rep from * to end.

Chart rnd 21: *Work right twist, work left twist, p2, ssk, k5, k2tog, p2; rep from * to end. 105 sts

Chart rnd 22: *K4, p2tog, k7, p2tog; rep from * to end. 91 sts

Chart rnd 23: *Work right twist, work left twist, p1, ssk, k3, k2tog, p1; rep from * to end. 77 sts

Chart rnd 24: *K2tog, ssk, p1, k5, p1; rep from * to end. 63 sts

Chart rnd 25: *K2, p1, ssk, k1, k2tog, p1; rep from * to end. 49 sts

Chart rnd 26: *K2tog, p1, Slk2togp, p1; rep from * to end. 28 sts

Chart rnd 27: *P2tog, k1, p1; rep from * to end. 21 sts

Chart rnd 28: *Slk2togp; rep from * to end. 7 sts

Finishing:
K7 remaining stitches on final round. Break yarn, leaving tail to weave in.

If making pom pom, leave extra length for fastening it to crown.

Weave in ends and block to size.

Make pom pom with remaining yarn and fasten to top of hat.

Chart

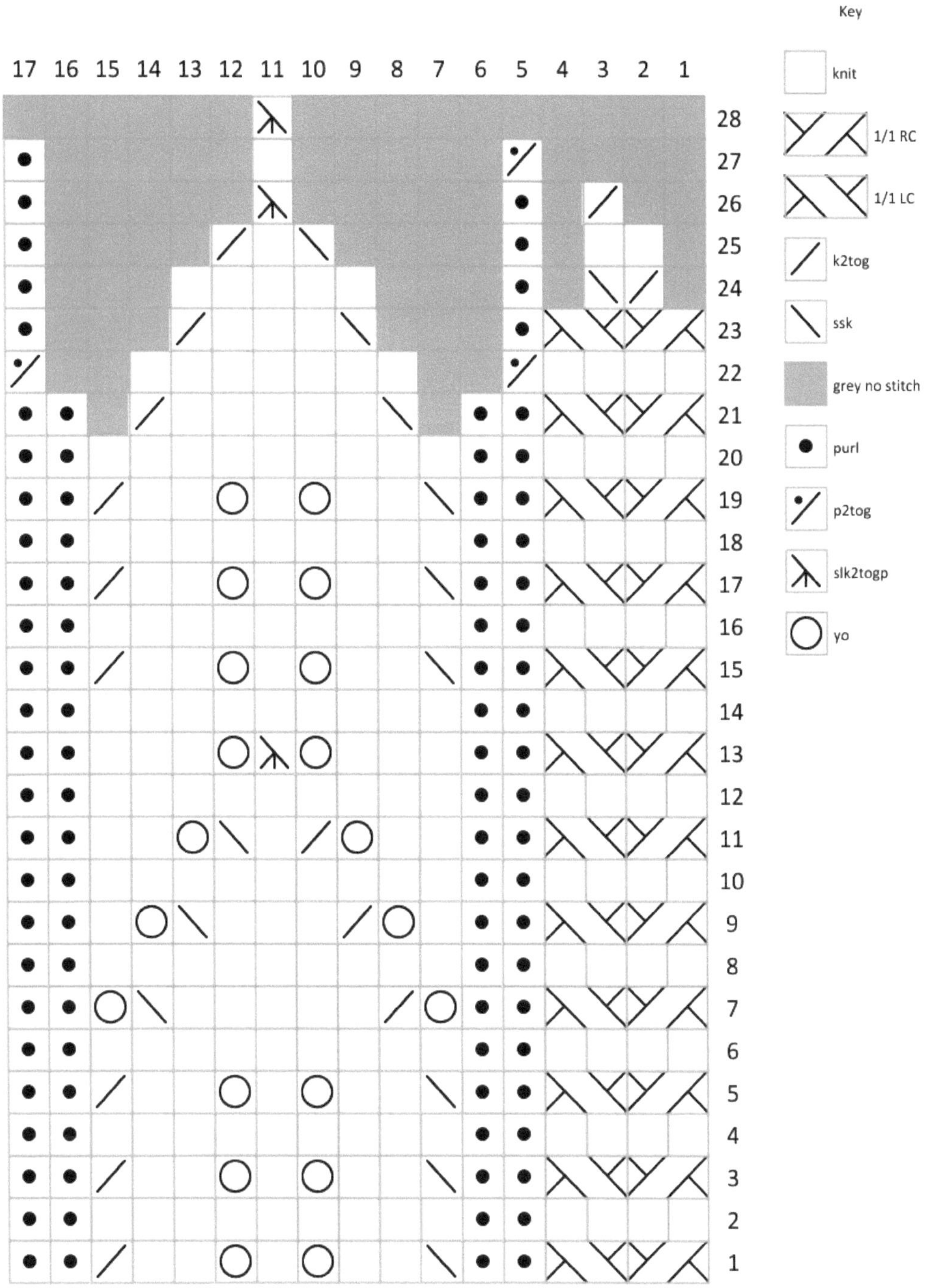

Key

- ☐ knit
- ╳ 1/1 RC
- ╳ 1/1 LC
- ╱ k2tog
- ╲ ssk
- ▓ grey no stitch
- ● purl
- ⩘ p2tog
- ⋏ slk2togp
- ○ yo

1/1LC (left twist) slip 1 st to cable needle and hold in front, k1, then k1 from cable needle
1/1RC (right twist) slip 1 st to cable needle and hold in back, k1, then k1 from cable needle

Hardcastle
Louise Tilbrook

Quick to work up in gloriously soft, squishy Whitfell DK, these fingerless mitts are ideal for a gift or as a treat for yourself. The bold, yet simple to knit cable runs up the back of the hand and the ribbed palm ensures a good fit with plenty of stretch. The pattern is available in three sizes and two lengths giving added versatility to this fantastic knit.

Materials

Eden Cottage Yarns Whitfell DK (DK, 50g; 100% baby Alpaca; 100m / 109yds per 50g ball)
Shade: Lichen; 1 (2) x 50g ball(s)

Needles and Accessories

One set of 3mm / US2.5 double pointed needles (or the size needed to obtain the correct gauge)

Note: Whilst cabling can be done without a needle, it is recommended that you use one here due to the complexity of the 5-stitch cables

Two stitch markers, waste yarn, cable needle, DPNs or preferred method of small circumference knitting

Sizes

S (M, L)

Finished circumference:
18 (22, 26)cm / 7 (8.75, 10.25)in

To fit: 17.5-20 (20-23, 24-27)cm / 7-8 (8-9, 9.5-10.5)in

The mitts can be worked in two lengths; standard 19cm / 7.5in and extra long, extending to fingertips, 22cm / 8.5in
Length: 19 (22)cm / 7.5 (8.5)in

Gauge

20 sts and 33 rows to 10cm (4in) in 2x2 rib on 3mm needles after blocking

Note: Adjust needle size if necessary to match gauge.

Pattern Notes

To work the RC/LC cables over 5 stitches, I recommend the use of a cable needle as follows:

2/1/2 LC: Sl 3st to cn and hold at front. k2 from LH needle. Sl p st from cn back to LH needle and purl it, k2 from cn.

2/1/2 RC: Sl 3st to cn and hold at back. k2 from LH needle. Sl p st from cn back to LH needle and purl it, k2 from cn.

Pattern

Right Mitt

Cast on 36 (44, 52) sts and join to work in the round, being careful not to twist sts, place marker to indicate beginning of rnd. Cable panel is worked over first 20 st using chart or written directions below, then work in k2, p2 rib to end of rnd.

Written Instructions for Cable Panel

Rnd 1-3: K2, p2, [k2, p1] 5 times, p1.
Rnd 4: K2, p2, k2, [p1, 2/1/2 LC] twice, p2.
Rnds 5-7: K2, p2, [k2, p1] 5 times, p1.
Rnd 8: K2, p2, [2/1/2 RC, p1] twice, k2, p2.

Work patt repeat 4 times, then set up increases for thumb gusset*.
Next rnd: Work cable panel as set, k2, p2, pm, k1, pm, k1, work in rib to end of rnd.

Work thumb increases as follows:

**Rnd 1: Work in patt to m, sm, kfbf, sm, work in patt to end of rnd, 2sts inc. 38 (46, 54)
Rnd 2: Work in patt to m, sm, k to m, sm, work in patt to end of rnd.
Rnd 3: Work in patt to m, sm, kfb, k to m, kfb, sm, work in patt to end of rnd, 2 sts inc. 40 (48, 56)

Repeat rnds 2 and 3 a further 4 times. 48 (56, 64) sts

On the next rnd, place the 13 gusset st onto waste yarn removing m as you come to them, k1, M1, work in patt to end. 35 (44, 52) sts
Work 2 further patt repeats then rib in patt (no further cabling) for 3cm (1.25in) for standard length and 6cm (2.5in) for extra long.
Cast off in rib.

Thumb

Slip 13 gusset st back onto needles and distribute evenly, M1 then join to work in the rnd. 14 sts
Knit plain for 3cm then switch to k1, p1 rib for 4 rnds. Cast off in rib.

Left Mitt

Work as for Right Mitt up until *

Set up increases for thumb gusset:

Work in est patt until 4 st before end of rnd, pm, k1, pm, k1, p2.

Work gusset increases as before from ** and cont as for right mitt.

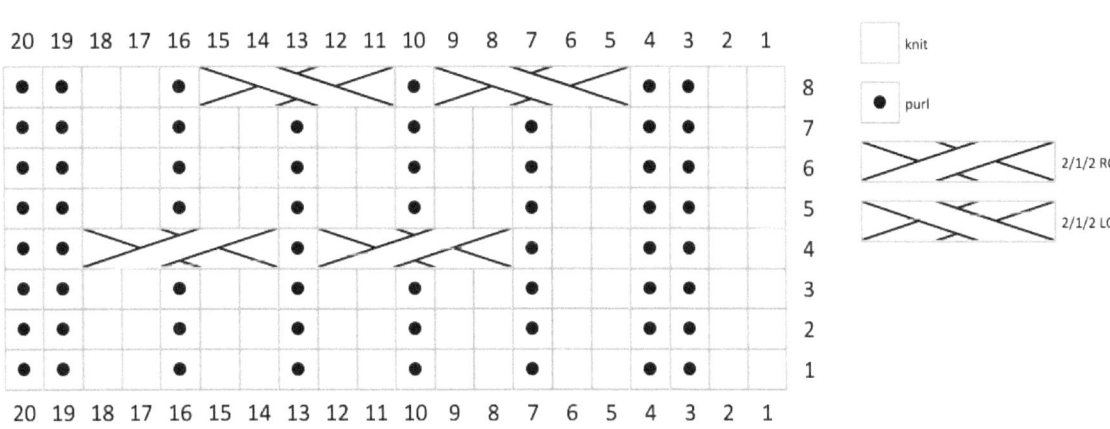

For cable stitches please refer to pattern notes above.

Deco Swirl
Louise Zass-Bangham

A statement cowl, heavily influenced by the rectilinear symmetry of Art Deco lines. Structural columns rotate round the neck, showing a more defined edge to this soft and fluffy Alpaca yarn. Make a neat, snug size for a quick gift, or go for the generous size for a more luxuriously snuggly version. Worked in the round, this is a straightforward knit.

Materials

Eden Cottage Yarns Whitfell DK (DK; 100% baby Alpaca; 100m / 109yds per 50g ball)
Snug shown in shade: Fuchsia; 2 (3) x 50g balls
Generous shown in shade: Laburnum; 2 (3) x 50g balls

Needles and Accessories

3.5mm (US 4) circular needles (or the size needed to obtain the correct gauge)
Snug size 40cm (16in) length for magic loop
Generous size 60cm (24in) length

Stitch markers (1 – 15 needed depending on marker placement)

Sizes

Snug (Generous)
Finished circumference: 50 (60)cm / 20 (24)in
Finished height: 22 (30)cm / 9 (12)in

Gauge

25 sts and 32 rows 10cm (4in) over stocking stitch, in the round, on 3.5mm needles after blocking.

Note: Adjust needle size if necessary to match gauge.

Pattern notes

Place a marker every 10 sts if you wish to mark each pattern repeat. Use a different coloured marker to mark the beginning of the round.

Pattern

Cast on 130 (150) sts and join to work in the round, being careful not to twist sts. Place marker to indicate beginning of rnd.

First border

Rnd 1: Knit, slipping markers on this and all following rnds.
Rnd 2: Purl.
Rnd 3: *M1, k4, k2tog, k4; rpt from * to end of rnd.
Rnd 4: Purl.
Rnds 5-10: Rpt rnds 3-4 three more times.
You should have 5 garter ridges.

Main pattern

Rnd 1: *M1, k4, k2tog, k4; rpt from * to end of rnd.
Rnd 2: Knit.
Rpt rnds 1-2 until work measures 19cm/8in (27cm/11in), measured from cast on edge.

Top border

Rnd 1: *M1, k4, k2tog, k4; rpt from * to end of rnd.
Rnd 2: Purl.
Rnds 3-10: Rpt rnds 3-10 four more times.
You should have 5 garter ridges.

Cast off loosely, knitwise.

Weave in ends and block to size.

Ja Ja
Åsa Tricosa

Large buttons, structural tailoring and a pop of eye-catching colour makes Ja Ja a perfect piece for every occasion. It will be as equally at home in a more formal environment as it will in a casual, laid-back affair. Adding a sharper, edgier element to the Drift Collection, this knitted jacket would be an excellent accompaniment to jeans and leather boots. Ja Ja is knitted with the Åsa Tricosa Ziggurat method: all in one go from top to bottom, not a seam in sight. Ja Ja is a challenging knit which will be oh-so-satisfying to wear.

Materials

Eden Cottage Yarns Whitfell DK (DK; 100% baby alpaca; 100m / 109yds per 50g ball)
MC Shade: Charcoal; 11 (12, 13, 14, 15) [16, 17, 18, 19, 19] x 50g balls
CC Shade: Lichen; 2 (2, 2, 2, 2) [3, 3, 3, 3, 3] x 50g balls

Needles and Accessories

3.5mm (US 4) circular needle, 80–100cm (32 - 40in) length (or the size needed to obtain the correct gauge)
3 mm (US 2) circular needle, 80–100cm (32 - 40in) length (or the size needed to obtain the correct gauge)

3 additional circular needles 3.5mm or smaller (any length)

Note: The additional circular needles are used for provisional cast ons, to set up the double knitted button bands, and to work the tuck

Waste yarn
Six stitch markers
3 buttons; 4cm (1.5in) diameter

Sizes

XS (S, M, L , XL) [2XL, 3XL, 4XL, 5XL, 6XL]

To fit: 81 (86, 91, 97, 102) [107, 112, 117, 122, 127]cm / 32 (34, 36, 38, 40) [42, 44, 46, 48, 50]in

Please refer to detailed schematic at the end of this pattern for more sizing details.

Gauge

22 sts and 28 rows to 10cm (4in) over stocking stitch on 3.5mm needles after blocking.

Note: Adjust needle size if necessary to match gauge.

Pattern Notes

Construction: From a regular cast on for the back, Ja Ja is knitted top-down, winding its way back and forth using Åsa's Top-Down Ziggurat Technique, with everything from cast on to cast off built-in and knitted as you go. The double-knitted front bands are cast on and knitted along with the rest. The sleeves can be knitted either using Magic Loop or on two circular needles. The back tuck is an unusual manoeuvre that requires some dexterity; an instruction for a simpler gather is provided as an alternative. A helpful table keeps track of rows and increases but is not required reading.

For best fit, choose size based on your back shoulder width less 1 cm / 0.25 in (see Upper Back in Schematic). Follow the instructions for that size through Step 6. Before working Step 7, take note of the difference between the number of final back sts in the size you're knitting and the size that corresponds to your ideal bust size. If your bust size is larger than the size you're knitting, add 1 round of body incs for every 2-stitch difference — begin them on an earlier row and/or make some every-row body incs. If your bust size is smaller than the size you're knitting, make fewer body incs (that is, start them later).

For wider hips: Increase more frequently after the straight waist rows, and/or add more sts across the back

Try your Ziggurat on every now and then! The beauty of top-down knitting is that you can try your garment for fit as you go.

Cast ons used: Longtail, Provisional Winding Cast On, Crochet Cast on.

German Short Rows for shoulder shaping: Wrap and turn — but without the wraps. On RS: after turning, sl 1^ (= sl 1 wyif and pull on yarn over and behind until stitch slips round and shows both its legs, k next st(s) as usual). When purling back over the sl 1^ on next WS (when you'd normally pick up the wraps), p1^ (= purl through both legs of the 'pulled-tight' st). On WS: after turning, sl 1^ (= sl 1 wyif, then pull down on yarn over/back of needle until the two legs of the st show on needle, purl next st(s) as usual). When knitting back over this stitch, k1^ (= knit the two legs of the st tog as if it were a normal, single st).

http://asatricosa.com/german-short-rows/

Sleeve cap and faux seam: All sts are more easily picked up from the RS, where you can see the result of the picking-up as you go. Sleeve-cap sts are picked up next to the slipped faux-seam sts. Where it says, pick up and purl, flip the work over and pick up and knit from RS to make sure the picked up st is adjacent to the faux seam and produces a nice visual line. Shoulder sts: the second st to be picked up is always picked up in line with (as a continuation of) the slipped faux seam. Note: before picking up shoulder sts, you'll need to loop the cable.

Double knitted buttonbands: Check your tension frequently to ensure even knitting. Cross yarns at the beginning of each dk section, at the end leave idle yarn (MC2/CC) hanging on WS.

Left Front
WS: With MC1 p to MC2 where double knitting section begins, bring MC2 to back, lay MC1 over MC2 and knit first dk st with MC2 (needle tip is crossing over MC1 to fetch MC2); p all MC1 sts, knit all MC2 sts.
RS: Cross MC2 over MC1 and knit first dk st with MC1 (needle tip is crossing over MC2); knit all MC1 sts, purl all MC2 sts.

Right Front
RS: With MC1 k to 1 st before first CC st, lay CC yarn over MC1, with MC1, k1 (needle tip is going over CC to fetch MC1), dk to end (knitting all MC1 sts, purling all CC sts); knit all MC1 sts, purl all CC sts.
WS: Cross MC1 over CC and knit first dk st with CC (needle tip is going over MC2), dk to end of section (purling all MC1 sts and knitting all CC sts), bring CC yarn to front (WS).

Drops Double Knitting Tutorial
https://vimeo.com/93305702

Double knitted pocket: Worked as buttonbands except on RS knit both layers, on WS purl both layers.

Making your yardage stretch: If you are cutting it close with your yarn, you can finish the sleeves before finishing the body. There's an indication in the pattern for this.

Pattern

STEP 1: Cast On and Right Back Shoulder

Using long-tail cast on and 3.5 mm needles, cast on 72 (74, 76, 80, 82) [86, 88, 90, 92, 94] sts.

Setup row (WS): P19 (20, 21, 22, 24) [25, 26, 26, 27, 28], turn.
Row 1 (RS): Sl 1^, PM, k11 (11, 13, 13, 15) [15, 15, 15, 17, 17], turn.
Row 2 (WS): Sl 1^, p to M, RM, p1^, p1, turn. 20 (21, 22, 23, 25) [26, 27, 27, 28, 29] shldr sts
Row 3: Sl 1^, PM, k6 (6, 7, 7, 8) [8, 8, 8, 9, 9], turn.
Row 4: Sl 1^, p to M, RM, p1^, p1, turn. 21 (22, 23, 24, 26) [27, 28, 28, 29, 30] shldr sts
Row 5: Sl 1^, PM, k to last 2 sts (working any sl 1^ as k1^), sl 1 wyib, k1.
Row 6: Purl to M, RM, p1^, p1, turn. 22 (23, 24, 25, 27) [28, 29, 29, 30, 31] shldrs sts
Row 7: Sl 1^, PM, k to last 2 sts, sl 1 wyib, k1.

Work Rows 6 & 7 once more. 23 (24, 25, 26, 28) [29, 30, 30, 31, 32] shldr sts
Next row (WS): P to M, RM, p1^, p to last 7 (7, 7, 8, 8) [9, 9, 9, 9, 10] sts, turn.

STEP 2: Left Back Shoulder

Row 1 (RS): Sl 1^, k11 (12, 13, 13, 15) [15, 16, 16, 17, 17], turn. 19 (20, 21, 22, 24) [25, 26, 26, 27, 28] shldr sts
Row 2 (WS): Sl 1^, PM, p6 (6, 7, 7, 8) [8, 8, 8, 9, 9], turn.
Row 3: Sl 1^, k to M, RM, k1^, k1, turn. 20 (21, 22, 23, 25) [26, 27, 27, 28, 29] shldr sts
Row 4: Sl 1^, PM, p to end (working any sl 1^ as p1^).
Row 5: K1, sl 1 wyib, k to M, RM, k1^, k1, turn. 21 (22, 23, 24, 26) [27, 28, 28, 29, 30] shldr sts
Row 6: Sl 1^, PM, p to end.

Work Rows 5 & 6 twice more. 23 (24, 25, 26, 28) [29, 30, 30, 31, 32] shldr sts

STEP 3: Working across Back and Shoulders

Row 1 (RS): K1, sl 1 wyib, k to M, RM, k1^, k to last 2 sts, sl 1 wyib, k1. 72 (74, 76, 80, 82) [86, 88, 90, 92, 94] sts
Row 2 (WS): Purl.
Row 3: K1, sl 1 wyib, k to last 2 sts, sl 1 wyib, k1.
Row 4: Purl.

Work Rows 3 & 4 1 (2, 3, 3, 3) [3, 3, 3, 4, 4] times more.

Continue to Step 4 without turning work.

STEP 4: Left Front Shoulder

After the shoulder sts have been picked up, wind on sts for the front using the working yarn and a provisional cast on that sets the double-knitted fronts. After a few rows, the double knitted neckband facing is closed and double knitting continues over only the 20 x 2 buttonband sts, and regular knitting continues over the front sts that are not part of the buttonband. See Hints & Tips for double knitting.

Setup Row (WS): PM, pick up and purl 6 (6, 7, 7, 7) [7, 7, 7, 8, 8] along edge (for first half of Left Sleeve Cap), loop cable, pick up and purl 18 (19, 20, 21, 23) [24, 25, 25, 26, 27] in the cast on of Left Back Shoulder. Remember to pick up second st in line with faux seam, place additional circular needle (N2) parallel to working needle (N1) to wind on 36 (37, 37, 39, 39) [41, 41, 43, 43, 44] sts.

Row 1 (RS): K wound sts on N1, PM, k12 (12, 12, 14, 14) [16, 16, 16, 16, 18], turn.

Row 2 (WS): Sl 1^, p to M, SM, p to end of N1, pull needle tip through so all sts rest on the cable; at M join new ball of MC (=MC2), k all sts on N2; transfer onto smaller circular needle (N3)—all sts from outer edge to M—alternately from N1 (knitted sts) & N2 (purled sts), starting with N1; this sets up the dk. 90 (93, 94, 99, 101) [106, 107, 111, 112, 115] sts

Row 3: With N1 and starting at far end, bring yarn of first st (MC1) under yarn of second st (=MC2); catching MC2 to knit first st with MC1, dk to M (k all MC1 sts, p all MC2 sts), sm; with MC1 k6 (6, 6, 7, 7) [8, 8, 8, 8, 9], turn.

Row 4: Sl 1^, p to M, SM, cross yarns, dk to end.

Row 5: Cross yarns, dk40, PM, with MC1, sskto M, RM, k to 2 sts before loop (working any sl 1^ as k1^), sl 1 wyib, k1, turn. 74 (76, 77, 80, 82) [85, 86, 88, 89, 91] sts

Row 6: P to M, SM, cross yarns, dk to end.

Row 7: Cross yarns, dk to M, SM, k to 2 sts before loop, sl 1 wyib, k1, turn.
Row 8: P to M, SM, cross yarns, dk to end.

Work Rows 7 & 8 4 (4, 5, 5, 5) [5, 5, 5, 6, 6] times more.

Work Row 7 once more. Continue to Step 5 without turning work.

STEP 5: Right Front Shoulder

Row 1 (RS): PM, pick up and knit 6 (6, 7, 7, 7) [7, 7, 7, 8, 8] (for second half of Left Sleeve Cap), k to M, SM, k1, sl 1 wyib, k to last 2 sts, sl 1 wyib, k1, PM, pick up and knit 6 (6, 7, 7, 7) [7, 7, 7, 8, 8] (for first half of Right Sleeve Cap), loop cable, pick up and knit 18 (19, 20, 21, 23) [24, 25, 25, 26, 27] in the cast on of Right Back Shoulder, with working yarn and additional circular needle (N2) wind on 36 (37, 37, 39, 39) [41, 41, 43, 43, 44] sts as for Left Front Shoulder.

Row 2: P all sts on N1, PM, p12 (12, 12, 14, 14) [16, 16, 16, 16, 18], turn.

Row 3: Sl 1^, k to M, SM, join new ball of MC (=MC3), k all sts on N1, pull N1 through so that all sts rest on the cable, with MC1 (at beg of cast on), p sts on N2 to last 20 sts, join CC, p20; transfer onto smaller circular needle (N3)—all sts from outer edge to M—alternately from N2 (knitted sts) & N1 (purled sts), starting with N2; this sets up the dk. 90 (93, 94, 99, 101) [106, 107, 111, 112, 115] sts

Row 4: Starting at outer edge, cross yarns, dk40 (k all CC, p all MC3), PM, cross CC over MC1 and continue with MC1 and MC3, dk to M (k all MC1, p all MC3), bring MC1 forward (to WS), SM, with MC3 p6 (6, 6, 7, 7) [8, 8, 8, 8, 9], turn.

Row 5: Sl 1^, k to M, SM, cross yarns, dk to M, SM, cross MC3 over CC, dk with CC and MC1 to end.
Row 6: Cross yarns, dk40, SM, with MC3 p2tog to M, RM, p to loop (working any sl 1^ as p1^), turn, break MC1 yarn. 74 (76, 77, 80, 82) [85, 86, 88, 89, 91] sts

Row 7: K1, sl 1 wyib, k to M, SM, dk as set.
Row 8: Dk40, p to loop, turn.

Work Rows 7 & 8 4 (4, 5, 5, 5) [5, 5, 5, 6, 6] times more.
Work Row 7 once more.

Next Row (WS): Dk40, p to 2 sts before loop, p2tog, PM, pick up and purl 6 (6, 7, 7, 7) [7, 7, 7, 8, 8] (for second half of Right Sleeve Cap), p to M, SM, ssp, p to 2 sts before M, p2tog, SM, p to M, SM, ssp, p to M, SM, dk as set to end. 73 (75, 76, 79, 81) [84, 85, 87, 88, 90] sts for each Front, 12 (12, 14, 14, 14) [14, 14, 14, 16, 16] Sleeve sts, 70 (72, 74, 78, 80) [84, 86, 88, 90, 92] Back sts

STEP 6: Sleeve Caps and Body Increases & Buttonholes

You will now increase for the sleeves and (later) body simultaneously. See also Helpful Table.

SLEEVE INCREASES

sM1 = sleeve increase

Row 1 (RS): Dk as set, SM, k to 1 st before M, sl 1 wyib, SM, sM1L, k to M, sM1R, SM, sl 1 wyib, k across back to 1 st before M, sl 1 wyib, SM, sM1L, k to M, sM1R, SM, sl 1 wyib, k to M, SM, dk as set. 14 (14, 16, 16, 16) [16, 16, 16, 18, 18] sts for each Sleeve

Row 2 (WS): Dk as set to M, SM, p to last M, SM, dk as set.

Work Rows 1 & 2 seven times more. 28 (28, 30, 30, 30) [30, 30, 30, 32, 32] Sleeve sts (for each Sleeve)

BUTTONHOLE

For the buttonhole the dk is worked with one yarn at a time; rows 2 & 3 are short rows and worked only over the buttonhole edge.

Buttonhole Row 1: Dk as set, k to 1 st before M, sl 1 wyib, SM, sM1L, k to M, sM1R, SM, sl 1 wyib, k across back to 1 st before M, sl 1 wyib, SM, sM1L, k to M, sM1R, SM, sl 1 wyib, k to M, SM, dk14, sl next (MC) st and leave MC hanging on WS, with CC p1, k2tog, BO, (k2tog, BO) 4 times (= 5 sts cast off), (sl 1 wyib, p1) to end. 30 (30, 32, 32, 32) [32, 32, 32, 34, 34] Sleeve sts

Buttonhole Row 2: (K1, sl 1 wyf) 7 times, k1, borrow last loop for crochet cast on to cast on 12 sts, replace borrowed loop on RH needle, turn.

Buttonhole Row 3: Leave CC hanging on WS, place last (MC) st on LH needle, with MC, ssk (the sl MC st and first CC st) , (sl 1 wyif, k1) 5 times, sl 1 wyif, k2tog (last cast-on CC st and first MC after cast on), (sl 1 wyif, k1) 5 times, sl 1 wyif, for next k1 fetch MC under CC bar between sts, sl 1 wyif, turn.

Buttonhole Row 4: (Sl 1 wyib, p1) 13 times, continue dk with MC & CC as set to M, SM, p to last M, SM, dk as set.

Work Rows 1 & 2 10 (10, 9, 10, 10) [10, 10, 10, 9, 8] times more. 50 (50, 50, 52, 52) [52, 52, 52, 52, 50] Sleeve sts

BODY INCREASES

Start Body Increases and continue with Sleeves Increases.
sM1 = sleeve inc   bM1 = body inc

Sizes 32 & 34 only
Make 2nd buttonhole over the next two rows below.

Row 3 (RS): Dk as set, SM, *k to 1 st before M, bM1L, sl 1 wyib, SM, sM1L, k to M, sM1R, SM, sl 1 wyib, bM1R,* work from * to * once more, k to M, SM, dk as set (with buttonhole for sizes 32 & 34).
52 (52, 52, 54, 54) [54, 54, 54, 54, 52] Sleeve sts, 74 (76, 77, 80, 82) [85, 86, 88, 89, 91] Front sts, 72 (74, 76, 80, 82) [86, 88, 90, 92, 94] Back sts

Row 4 (WS): Dk as set to M, SM, p to last M, SM, dk as set.

Sizes 36, 38, 40, 42, 44, 46 only
Make 2nd buttonhole over the next two rows below.

Size 48 & 50 only
Make 2nd buttonhole over two rows; for size 48 on 2nd repeat, for size 50 on 3rd repeat of Rows 3 & 4 below.

Work Rows 3 & 4 1 (1, 2, 1, 1) [1, 2, 3, 4, 4] time(s) more. 54 (54, 56, 56, 56) [56, 58, 60, 62, 60] Sleeve sts, 75 (77, 79, 81, 83) [86, 88, 91, 93, 95] Front sts, 74 (76, 80, 82, 84) [88, 92, 96, 100, 102] Back sts

Size 32: Skip to ****
Size 48: Skip to ***

Row 5: As Row 3. – (56, 58, 58, 58) [58, 60, 62, –, 62] Sleeve sts, – (78, 80, 82, 84) [87, 89, 92, –, 96] Front sts, – (78, 82, 84, 86) [90, 94, 98, –, 104] Back sts

Row 6: Dk as set to M, SM, *p to 1 st before M, bM1Rp, p1, SM, k to M, SM, k1, bM1Lp,* work from * to * once more, p to M, SM, dk as set. – (79, 81, 83, 85) [88, 90, 93, –, 97] Front sts, – (80, 84, 86, 88) [92, 96, 100, –, 106] Back sts

Work Rows 5 & 6 – (0, 0, 1, 2) [2, 2, 1, –, 2] time(s) more. – (56, 58, 60, 62) [62, 64, 64, –, 66] Sleeve sts, – (79, 81, 84, 87) [90, 92, 94, –, 97] Front sts, – (80, 84, 90, 96) [100, 104, 104, –, 114] Back sts

***

Size 46, 48, 50 only
Row 7: Dk as set, SM, *k to 1 st before M, bM1L, sl 1 wyib, SM, k to M, SM, sl 1 wyib, bM1R,* work from * to * once more, k to M, SM, dk as set. - (-, -, -, -) [-, -, 64, 62, 66] Sleeve sts, - (-, -, -, -) [-, -, 95, 94, 100] Front sts, - (-, -, -, -) [-, -, 106, 102, 116] Back sts
Row 8: As Row 6. - (-, -, -, -) [-, -, 64, 62, 66] Sleeve sts, - (-, -, -, -) [-, -, 96, 95, 101] Front sts, - (-, -, -, -) [-, -, 108, 104, 118] Back sts

Size 48 only
Work Rows 5 – 8 once more. 64 Sleeve sts, 99 Front sts, 112 Back sts

****

All sizes

Work Rows 3 & 4 once. 56 (58, 60, 62, 64) [64, 66, 66, 66, 68] Sleeve sts, 76 (80, 82, 85, 88) [91, 93, 97, 100, 102] Front sts, 76 (82, 86, 92, 98) [102, 106, 110, 114, 120] Back sts

STEP 7: Separating Sleeves and Body

Sep Row 1 (RS): Dk as set, SM, *k to 2 sts before M, PM, k2, RM, put all sts to next M on holder, (= sleeve sts) RM, (flip work over so WS is facing) borrow last st for cast on loop,* crochet cast on 9 (9, 9, 10, 10) [11, 11, 12, 13, 13] sts, PM, cast on 6 (6, 6, 7, 7) [8, 8, 9, 10, 10] sts, replace remaining loop onto LH needle, flip work over so RS is facing, work from * to * once more, crochet cast on 10 (10, 10, 11, 11) [12, 12, 13, 14, 14], PM, cast on 5 (5, 5, 6, 6) [7, 7, 8, 9, 9], replace remaining loop onto LH needle, flip work over so RS is facing, k to M, SM, dk as set.

84 (88, 90, 94, 97) [101, 103, 108, 112, 114] Left Front sts, 82 (86, 88, 92, 95) [99, 101, 106, 110, 112] Right Front sts, 92 (98, 102, 110, 116) [122, 126, 132, 138, 144] Back sts

Sep Row 2: Dk as set, SM, *p to 1 st before cast on, sl 1, make twisted loop in cast on bar and place on LH needle, sl 1 to LH needle, p2tog (loop and sl st), p to M, SM, k1, p to M, RM, ssp,* work from * to * once more, p to last M, SM, dk as set.

83 (87, 89, 93, 96) [100, 102, 107, 111, 113] Left Front, 82 (86, 88, 92, 95) [99, 101, 106, 110, 112] Right Front, 91 (97, 101, 109, 115) [121, 125, 131, 137, 143] Back sts

Continue in stocking st on body sts only (setting sleeve sts to the side) working Buttonbands as set and make the third (final) buttonhole.

Note: A faux side seam is created along each side by, on WS, knitting the st after each side M. This stitch is not included in the stitch counts that follow. 82 (86, 88, 92, 95) [99, 101, 106, 110, 112] sts for each Front, 90 (96, 100, 108, 114) [120, 124, 130, 136, 142] Back sts.

STEP 8: Tuck

You will create three layers that are worked in a zig-zag mode, for which you need several help needles. Use extra circulars so that resting sts can be slid onto their cables.

The instructions are for 5 needles — you can make do with fewer by looping the cables but I don't know how to describe the moves with fewer needles. Work the sts on each needle with that same needle.

Tuck Row 1 (RS): Dk as set, SM, k to M, SM, k41 (44, 46, 50, 53) [56, 58, 61, 64, 67], *kfb 5 times, place the 5 created sts (every other stitch; the ones knitted into the back legs) on a separate circular needle held behind working needle (N1),* work from * to * once more, k to last M, SM, dk as set.

The first extra needle is N2, the second is N3. You have two layers and will now create a third. 100 (106, 110, 118, 124) [130, 134, 140, 146, 152] Back sts

Tuck Row 2 (WS): Dk as set, SM, p to M, SM, k1, p to first set of kfb sts, from N3 work from * to * but place the created 5 sts on N4 in front of the work.

You have three layers of sts on separate needles for the first half of the tuck.
The working yarn is at the end of N4 which sits on top.
N3 holds 5 sts and sits between N4 and N1.
From N2 (kfb) 5 times, place the created 5 sts on N5 in front of N2 and N1.
The working yarn is at the end of N5.
Slide sts on N5 to end of N4 (discard N5). There are 10 sts on N4.
Flip work around (to work from RS), p5 from N2 (the middle needle).
Flip work around (to work from WS again).

Working with N1, slip 5 sts to RH needle, p to M, SM, k1, p to M, SM, dk as set.
The sts on N1 are divided in two — with the tuck developing in the middle. 110 (116, 120, 128, 134) [140, 144, 150, 156, 162] Back sts

Tuck Row 3: Dk as set, k to centre back (= end of first half of N1).
Flip work to work from WS, on and with N2, k5.
Flip work to work from RS, on and with N4, k10.
Flip work to work from WS, on and with N3, k5.
Flip work to work from RS, on and with N1 (second half), k to last M, SM, dk as set.

Row 4: Dk as set, p to M, SM, k1, p to centre (= end of first half of N1).
Flip work to work from RS, on and with N3 (middle needle), p5.
Flip work to work from WS, on and with N4, p10.
Flip work to work from RS, on and with N3, p5.
Flip work to work from WS, on and with N1 (second half), p to M, SM, k1, p to M, SM, dk as set.

Alternative Simple Gather (in lieu of Tuck)
Gather Row 1 (RS): Dk as set, k to M, sm k41 (44, 46, 50, 53) [56, 58, 61, 64, 67], (kfb) 10 times, PM, k to last M, SM, dk as set. 100 (106, 110, 118, 124) [130, 134, 140, 146, 152] Back sts

Gather Row 2 (WS): Dk as set, p to M, SM, k1, p to M, RM, (p1, kfb) 10 times, p to Ms, SM, k1, p to M, dk as set. 110 (116, 120, 128, 134) [140, 144, 150, 156, 162] Back sts

Gather Row 3: Dk as set, k to last M, SM, dk as set.
Gather Row 4: Dk as set, p to M, SM, k1, p to M, SM, k1, p to M, SM, dk as set.

Work Tuck (or Gather) Rows 3 & 4 5 (4, 4, 5, 4) [4, 3, 2, 2, 2] times more.

Work Rows 3 & 4 once more and make the third (final) buttonhole over these two rows.

Work Rows 3 & 4 0 (0, 0, 0, 0) [0, 2, 4, 4, 4] times more. 276 (290, 298, 314, 326) [340, 348, 364, 378, 388] sts, incl side g sts (2)

STEP 9: A-Line Shaping

The next row sets up the increases for the A-Line shaping, you will place two markers for the central increases (bringing the marker total to six).

If working **TUCK**, work all sts with N1, placing a stitch marker on either side of the centre 10 tuck stitches as you work them onto N1, making a loop or two in the cable if necessary, and removing all extra needles.

If working **GATHER** place the markers either side of the centre 10 gather stitches.

Stitch counts that foll include side g sts (2).

Increase Row (RS): Dk as set, **SM**, k to 1 st before side seam marker, M1R, k1, **SM**, M1L, k to **centre 10 TUCK** stitches, **PM**, M1R, k10, M1L, **SM** k to 1 st before side seam marker, M1R, k1, **SM**, M1L, k to M, **SM**, dk as set. 282 (296, 304, 320, 332) [346, 354, 370, 384, 394] sts

Row 2 (WS): Dk as set, SM, p to side seam M, SM, k1, p to side seam M, SM, k1, p to M, SM, dk as set.
Row 3: Dk as set, SM, k to M, SM, dk as set.
Row 4: As Row 2.

Work rpts of Rows 3 & 4, and rpt increase row (slipping instead of placing markers) on every 14th row 3 times more, then once on every 16th, then on every 18th row.

NOTE: If you are trying to stretch your yardage precisely, this is the place to set the body aside and work the sleeves before finishing the body. If so, work Steps 13 –15 first.

Work to 21 (21, 22, 22, 22) [22, 22, 22, 23, 23] cm or 8.25 (8.25, 8.75, 8.75, 8.75) [8.75, 8.75, 8.75, 9, 9] in from underarm.

STEP 10: Double-Knitted Pockets

If you wish you can knit a simpler inline pocket — if choosing this alternative, skip to Step 10B now.

For the first few rows each opening is flanked by 3 sts on either side. On RS these are worked as k1, sl 1 wyif, k1 – where the sl 1 on the first row is an increase between the two knitted sts, on WS the 3 sts are worked as sl 1 wyif, k1, sl 1 wyif.

After six rows, the outmost k1 is ssk/k2tog with the centre st.

Row 1 (RS): Dk as set, SM, k10 (10, 10, 12, 12) [14, 14, 16, 18, 18], *PM, k1, M1L, k1, Crochet Cast On 24 sts with working yarn. Set aside for now.

With spare 3.5 mm needle, join CC, k23 (parallel to the cast on and continuing on body sts as if you hadn't cast on anything), set aside.

Continue with MC (where you ended with CC – and catch CC with MC for normal intarsia 'join', that is, bring MC up under CC): K1, M1L, k1, PM,* k to 37 (37, 37, 39, 39) [41, 41, 43, 45, 45] sts before last M, work from * to * once more, k to M, SM, dk as set.

Row 2 (WS): Dk as set, SM, *p to M, SM, sl 1 wyif, k1, sl 1 wyif, begin double knitting, that is, work 1 st alternately from spare needle and from main needle as follows:

Bring CC and MC to back , lay MC over CC, bring CC to front, purl CC and hold yarn to front, with LH needle pick up twisted loop of cast-on bar, with MC k2tog, (p CC, k MC) to last cast-on MC-stitch, work last MC with next MC (the first st of the 3 edging sts) as an ssp, k1, sl 1 wyif, sm,** (p to side M, SM, k1) twice, work from * to * once more, p to M, SM, work dk as set.
All sts are now on one needle.

Continue double knitting over the pockets, catching CC only at beginning of each pocket on each row, that is, right after the 3 edge sts. Continue with A-line shaping as set.

Row 1 (RS): Work dk as set, SM, *k to first pocket M, SM, k1, sl 1 wyif, k1, cross yarns, dk the 23 pocket sts (k1 alternately with MC and CC 23 times), k1, sl 1 wyif, k1, sm,* work from * to * once more, k to last M, SM, work dk as set.

Row 2 (WS): Work dk as set, SM, *p to M, SM, sl 1 wyif, k1, sl 1 wyif, cross yarns, dk the pocket sts (p1 CC , k1 MC), with MC sl 1 wyif, k1, sl 1 wyif, sm,* (p to side M, SM, k1) twice, work from * to * once more, p to last M SM, work dk as set.

From this point forward:
On RS rows knit all pocket sts (MC & CC).
On WS rows purl all pocket sts (MC & CC).

Row 3: As Row 1
Row 4: Work dk as set, SM, *p to M, SM, sl 1 wyif, k1, sl 1 wyif, cross yarns, dk the pocket sts (p CC, p MC), with MC sl 1 wyif, k1, sl 1 wyif, sm,* (p to side M, SM, k1) twice, work from * to * once more, p to last M, SM, work dk as set.

Work Rows 3 & 4 once more.

Row 7: Work dk as set, SM, *k to first pocket M, RM, ssk, k1, PM, cross yarns, dk the 23 pocket sts (k1 alternately with MC and CC 23 times), PM, k1, k2tog, RM,* work from * to * once more, k to last M, SM, work dk as set.
Row 8: Work dk as set, SM, *p to M, SM, cross yarns, dk the pocket sts (p1 alternately with CC and MC), with MC, sm,* (p to side M, SM, k1) twice, work from * to * once more, p to last M, SM, work dk as set.
Row 9: Work dk as set, SM, *k to first pocket M, SM, cross yarns, double knit the 23 pocket sts (k1 alternately with MC and CC 23 times), SM,* work from * to * once more, k to last M, SM, work dk as set.
Row 10: As Row 8.

Rept Rows 9 & 10 until pocket measures 10 cm / 4 in from cast on.

Next Row (RS): Work dk as set, SM, *k to first pocket M, RM, knit the two pocket layers together as follows: With MC, using one MC- st and one CC lining-st (in that order) ssk 23 times, RM, cut CC,* work from * to * once more, k to last M, SM, work dk as set.

STEP 10b: Inline Pockets

Next Row (RS): Work dk as set, SM, k13 (13, 13, 15, 15) [17, 17, 19, 21, 21], *join short piece of waste yarn and k23, slip these 23 sts back to LH needle, with working yarn knit same 23 sts again,* k to side M, SM, k to 26 (26, 26, 26, 26) [28, 28, 28, 30, 30] before last M, work from * to * once more, k to last M, SM, work dk as set. Pocket linings are worked later in Step 16.

STEP 11: After the Pockets

Continue to work in st st with dk buttonbands and A-line shaping as set.

Work to 38.5 (39, 39.5, 40, 41) [41.5, 41.5, 41.5, 41.5] cm or 15.25 (15.25, 15.50, 15.75, 16.25) [16.25, 16.25, 16.25, 16.25,16.25] in from underarm or to 3 cm (1.25 in) from desired length, and ending with a WS row.

STEP 12: Hem

Change to smaller (3 mm) needle.
Row 1 (RS): Dk as set, SM, *with nearside MC k1, with farside MC k1 into bar between sts, rpt from * to last M, SM, dk with MC & CC as set.
Rows 2 – 6: Dk across all sts (k nearside sts, purl farside sts as set in buttonbands but now across all sts), cut CC.
Rows 7 & 8: As Rows 2– 6 but with MC only.
Cast off from RS: ssk *ssk, BO, work from * end. Cut yarn, pull yarn through rem st.

STEP 13: Right Sleeve

Work sleeves in the round (either on 2 circulars or with the Magic Loop method).
Put 56 (58, 60, 62, 64) [64, 66, 66, 66, 68] Right Sleeve sts from holder back on larger (3.5 mm) needle. Attach MC at right-hand side of gap, pick up and knit 6 (6, 6, 7, 7) [8, 8, 9, 10, 10] along the first half of the cast-on underarm sts, PM, pick up and knit 7 (7, 7, 8, 8) [9, 9, 10, 11, 11] along second half of underarm, k to M. 69 (71, 73, 77, 79) [81, 83, 85, 87, 89] sts

Work in st st for 5 cm / 2 in, then begin sleeve decreases.

Sleeve Decreases:
Next Rnd/Sleeve-Decrease Rnd: SM, work 1 g st, k2tog, k to 2 sts before M, SSK.

Rpt Sleeve-Decrease Rnd every 17 (17, 16, 14, 14) [14, 14, 14, 12, 12]th round 6 (6, 7, 8, 8) [8, 8, 8, 9, 9] times more. 55 (57, 57, 59, 61) [63, 65, 67, 67, 69] sts

Work to 45 (45, 46, 46, 47) [47, 47, 47, 47, 47] cm / 17.50 (17.50, 18, 18, 18.50) [18.50, 18.50, 18.50, 18.50, 18.50] in from underarm or to desired length.

STEP 14: Upturned Double Cuff

The curved cuff is double with each layer knit separately and joined using a 3-needle cast off.

Change to smaller (3 mm) needle).
Rnd 1: *K1, yo, to end.
Transfer all yo to a separate circular needle (N2) on the inside of the working circular (N1). Leave these sts aside for now.

Rnds 2 – 6: Knit.
Begin short row shaping.
Row 7 (RS): K to last 4 (4, 4, 2, 2) [4, 4, 4, 4, 4] sts, turn.
Row 8 (WS): Sl 1^, PM, p to last 4 (4, 4, 2, 2) [4, 4, 4, 4, 4] sts, turn.
Row 9: Sl 1^, PM, k to 3 sts before M, turn.
Row 10: Sl 1^, PM, p to 3 sts before M, turn.
Work Rows 9 – 10 4 (4, 4, 5, 5) [5, 5, 5, 5, 5] times more.

Next rnd: Sl 1^, PM, k to beginning of round M, removing Ms as you go and working any sl 1^ (the first st after each M) as k1^, do not turn.
Continue in the round (RS).

Next rnd: (RS): K to end of round, removing Ms as you go and working any sl 1^ (the st before each M) as k1^. Leave sts aside for now.

Join CC and use smaller (3 mm) needle. Fold the sts on N1 outward to make N2 available. Work the sts on N2 from the inside (knitting in the opposite direction of outer cuff) to create the double cuff.
Knit 1 round, purl 1 round.
Work Rnds/Rows 2 – 18.

Fold up sts on N1 so that N1 & N2 are parallel. With CC and working from the inside, cast off all sts using a 3-needle cast off.

STEP 15: Left Sleeve

Work as Right Sleeve.

STEP 16: Inline Pocket Linings

From RS, pick up 23 sts below and 23 sts above waste yarn without knitting them. Remove waste yarn. 46 sts With smaller needle join CC at right side of sts below the opening, k23 (to end of lower edge sts), pick up and knit 1 in 'edge' st, loop, k23 along top edge, pick up and knit 1 in 'edge' st, loop. 48 sts
Rnd 1: P24, loop, k23, p1, loop.
Rnd 2: (K24, loop) twice.
Rnd 3: Knit.
Work Rnds 2 & 3 until pocket measures 10 cm / 4 in. Turn pocket outside in and close with a 3-needle cast off.

Finish

Weave in loose ends. Soak and block to measurements.

Turn up cuffs.

Sew on Buttons.

Schematic

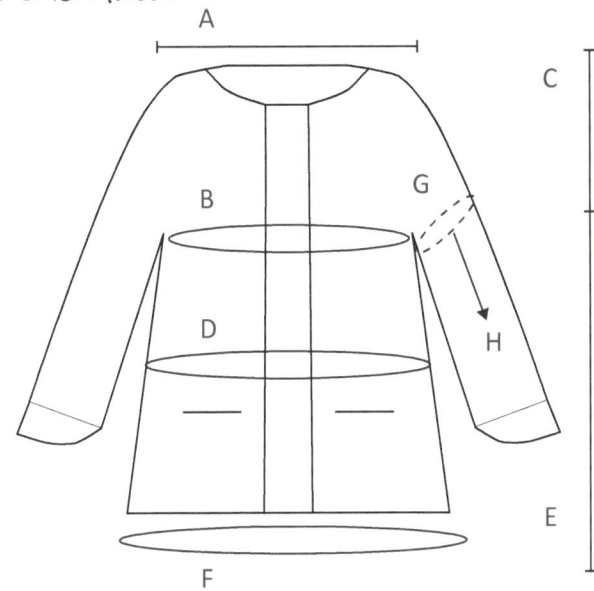

A) Upper Back: 32 (32.5, 33.5, 35.5, 36.5) [38, 39, 40, 41, 42]cm / 12.5 (12.75, 13.25, 14, 14.25) [15, 15.25, 15.75, 16.25, 16.5]in

B) Bust: 82 (87.5, 91, 98, 103.5) [109, 112.5, 118, 123.5, 129]cm / 32.25 (34.5, 35.75, 38.5, 40.75) [43, 44.25, 46.5, 48.5, 50.75]in

C) Armhole depth: 20.5 (21.5, 22, 23, 23.5) [23.5, 24.5, 25, 25.5, 25.5]cm
8.25 (8.5, 8.75, 9.25, 9.5) [9.5, 9.75, 10, 10.25, 10.25]in

D) Waist: 134 (145, 148.5, 156, 161.5) [168, 172, 179, 185.5, 190.5]cm
52.75 (57, 58.5, 61.5, 63.75) [66.25, 67.75, 70.5, 73, 75]in

E) Total length: 56 (57, 58, 59, 60) [61, 62, 62, 63, 63]cm
22 (22.5, 22.75, 23.25, 23.5) [24, 24.5, 24.5, 24.75, 24.75]in

F) Bottom Hem Circumference: 110 (116, 119.5, 126.5, 132.5) [138.5, 142, 147.5, 153, 158.5]cm / 42.25 (44.5, 45.75, 48.5, 50.75) [53, 54.25, 56.5, 58.75, 60.75]in

G) Sleeve Circumference at top: 31.5 (32.5, 33, 35, 36) [37, 37.5, 38.5, 39.5, 40.5]cm / 12.5 (12.75, 13, 13.75, 14.25) [14.5, 14.75, 15.25, 15.5, 16]in

H) Sleeve Seam: 45 (45, 46, 46, 47) [47, 47, 47, 47, 47]cm / 17.75 (17.75, 18, 18, 18.5) [18.5, 18.5, 18.5, 18.5, 18.5]in

Beulah
Clare Devine

When a cold, blustery day calls for a touch of cosy style, Beulah delivers. This relaxed fit beanie features a detailed lace cable flowing along the side, providing pretty detail in this feminine design. The soft, luxurious Whitfell DK complements the hat beautifully, ensuring you'll be snug no matter what the weather throws at you.

Materials

Eden Cottage Yarns Whitfell DK (DK; 100% baby Alpaca; 100m / 109yds per 50g ball)
Shade: Misty Woods; 2 x 50g balls
Sample shown in Steel on page 20.

Needles and Accessories

3.25mm (US3) circular needle, 40cm (16in) length (or the size needed to obtain the correct gauge)
One set of 3.25mm / US3 double pointed needles

A long circular needle 80cm (32in) may be used for the magic loop method, removing the need for DPNs.

Five stitch markers
Darning needle
Cable Needle

Sizes

Small (medium, large)
Finished circumference:
44 (48, 52)cm / 17.5 (19, 20.5)in

To fit: 50 (55, 60)cm / 20 (22, 24)in
Length from brim to crown:
22 (22.5, 23)cm / 8.75 (9, 9.25)in

Gauge

24 sts and 32 rounds to 10cm (4in) over stocking stitch on 3.25mm needles after blocking.

Note: Adjust needle size if necessary to match gauge.

The lace panel varies in width and has therefore not been included for gauge. Round gauge in particular is important for determining the overall length – too loose a round gauge might give you an oversized hat.

Pattern Notes

Over rounds 11 to 39 you steadily increase and then decrease stitches giving the hat a lovely shape and framing the lace insert in the cable panel. The stitch counts for the cable panel are shown in the written instructions. It may help you to place a marker at either side of the cable panel in round one if you wish to keep track of these increases.

Pattern

Cast on 104 (114, 124) sts and join to work in the rnd, being careful not to twist sts. Place marker to indicate beginning of rnd. Use a stretchy cast on such as the German Twisted or Long Tail Cast On.

Brim

Rnd 1: (K3tbl, p2), 16 (18, 20) times, k3tbl, p1, then *k3tbl, p2; rpt from * to end of rnd.

Rpt this rnd another 9 times.

Body

Set up: K78 (88, 98), pm. This is now the start of your rnd.

It may help to place a marker at the end of the cable panel in round one, after 11sts. This will help you keep track of the increases. See pattern notes for details.

Rnds 1 - 37: Work from chart or written instructions, then k to end of rnd.

Crown

Rnd 38: Work from chart or written instructions, k9 (11, 13). This is now the start of your rnd.

On the next rnd you will place a number of markers. Markers A, B and C are to keep track of the crown decreases. Marker D shows the start of the charted section and you should also have a fifth BOR marker in place.

Rnd 39: K25 (27, 29), pm(A), k25 (27, 29), pm(B), k25 (27, 29) pm(C), k9 (11, 13) pm(D), work from chart or written instructions, knit to end of rnd.

Rnd 40 and all odd rnds: (K1, ssk, k to 3 sts before m, k2tog, k1, sm) three times; k1, ssk, k to m(D), work from chart or written instructions, k to 3 sts before end of rnd, k2tog, k1. 8 sts dec.

Rnd 41 and all even rnds: K to m(D), work from chart or written instructions, k to end of rnd.

Work these two rnds, continuing with chart as set, 8 more times. 32 (42, 52) sts

Then work final crown decreases for relevant size. m(D) is no longer required and can be removed on round 1.

Small

Rnd 1: (K1, ssk, k1, k2tog, k1) x 3, k1, ssk twice, k1, k2tog twice, k1. 22 sts
Rnd 2: (K1, s2kpo, k1) x 3, k1, ssk, k1, k2tog, k1. 14 sts
Rnd 3: S2kpo x 3, k1, s2kpo, k1. 6 sts

Medium

Rnd 1: (K1, ssk, k to 3 sts before m, k2tog, k1, sm) three times; k1, ssk, p1, k7, p1, k2tog, k1. 34 sts
Rnd 2: (K1, ssk, k1, k2tog, k1, sm) three times; k1, ssk, k7, k2tog, k1. 26 sts

Large

Rnd 1: (k1, ssk, k to 3 sts before m, k2tog, k1, sm) three times; k1, ssk, k1, p2, k7, p2, k1, k2tog, k1. 44 sts
Rnd 2: (K1, ssk, k3, k2tog, k1, sm) three times; k1, ssk, p2, k7, p2, k2tog, k1. 36 sts
Rnd 3: (K1, ssk, k1, k2tog, k1, sm) three times; k1, ssk, p1, k7, p1, k2tog, k1. 28 sts
Rnd 4: Knit to m(C), k1, ssk, k to 2 sts before end of rnd, k2tog, k1. 26sts

Medium and Large

Next rnd (Both sizes): (K1, s2kpo, k1) x 3, k1, ssk twice, k1, k2tog twice, k1. 16 sts
Final rnd (Both sizes): S2kpo x 3, k1, ssk, k1, k2tog, k1. 8 sts

Break yarn and thread through remaining live stitches using a tapestry needle. Draw to close and weave in ends. Block the hat over a balloon.

Written Instructions

Rnd 1: P2, 3/1/3 RC, p2. 11 sts
Rnds 2 - 8: P2, k7, p2.
Rnd 9: P2, 3/1/3 RC, p2. 11 sts
Rnd 10: P2, k7, p2.
Rnd 11: P2, k3, yo, k, yo, k3, p2. 13 sts
Rnd 12: P2, k9, p2.
Rnd 13: P2, (k3, yo) x 2, k3, p2. 15 sts
Rnd 14: P2, k11, p2.
Rnd 15: P2, k3, yo, k5, yo, k3, p2. 17 sts
Rnd 16: P2, k13, p2.
Rnd 17: P2, k3, yo, k2, k2tog, (yo, k3) x 2, p2. 19 sts
Rnd 18: P2, k15, p2.
Rnd 19: P2, k3, yo, k2, k2tog, yo, k1tbl, yo, ssk, k2, yo, k3, p2. 21 sts
Rnd 20: P2, k17, p2.
Rnd 21: P2, k3, yo, k2tog x 2, yo, k3, yo, ssk x 2, yo, k3, p2.
Rnd 22: P2, k17, p2.
Rnd 23: P2, k3, yo, k2tog, k2, yo, s2kpo, yo, k2, ssk, yo, k3, p2.
Rnds 24 - 27: Rpt rnds 20 - 23.
Rnd 28: P2, k17, p2.
Rnd 29: P2, k3, yo, k2tog x 2, yo, k3, yo, ssk x 2, yo, k3, p2.
Rnd 30: P2, k17, p2.
Rnd 31: P2, k2, ssk, yo, k2tog, k, yo, s2kpo, yo, k, ssk, yo, k2tog, k2, p2. 19 sts
Rnd 32: P2, k15, p2.
Rnd 33: P2, k2, ssk, yo, k2tog, k3, ssk, yo, k2tog, k2, p2. 17 sts
Rnd 34: P2, k13, p2.
Rnd 35: P2, k2, ssk, yo, k2tog, k, ssk, yo, k2tog, k2, p2. 15 sts
Rnd 36: P2, k11, p2.
Rnd 37: P2, k2, ssk, yo, s2kpo, yo, k2tog, k2, p2. 13 sts
Rnd 38: P2, k9, p2.
Rnd 39: P2, k3, s2kpo, k3, p2. 11 sts
Rnd 40: P2, 3/1/3 RC, p2. 11 sts
Rnd 41 - 47: P2, k7, p2.
Rnd 48: P2, 3/1/3 RC, p2. 11 sts
Rnds 49 - 55: P2, k7, p2.
Rnd 56: P2, 3/1/3 RC, p2. 11 sts
Rnd 57: P2, k7, p2.

Chart

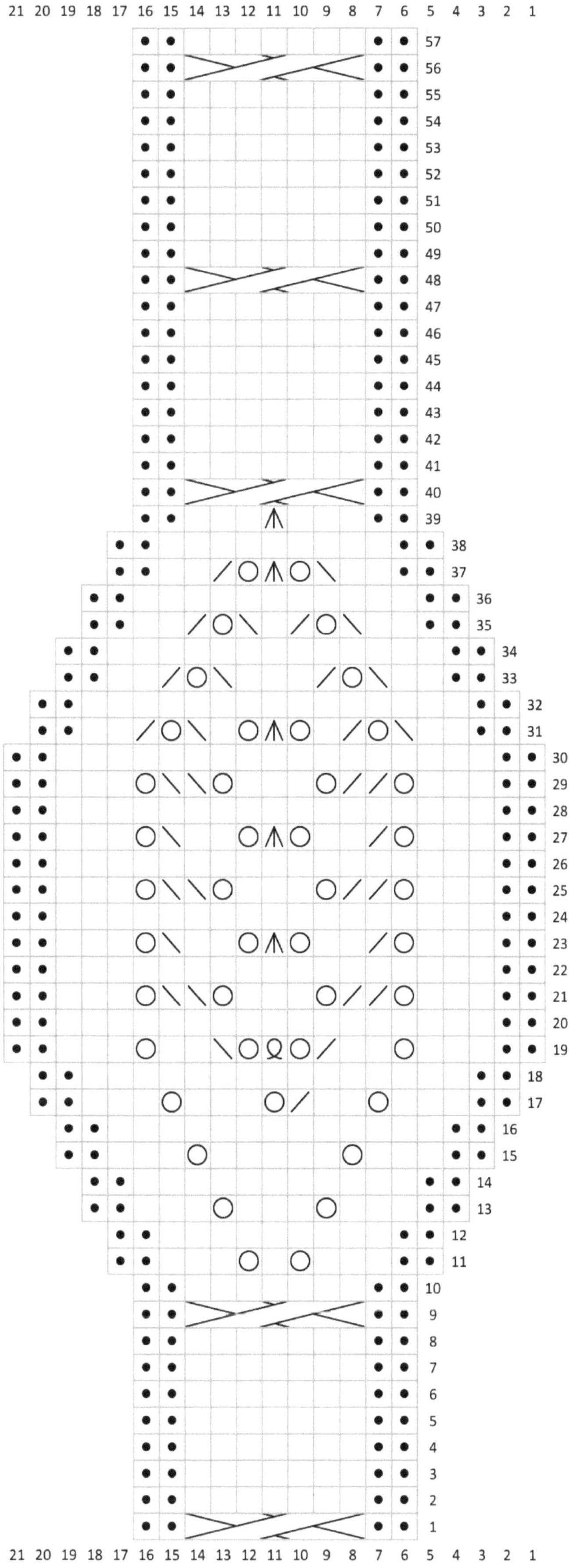

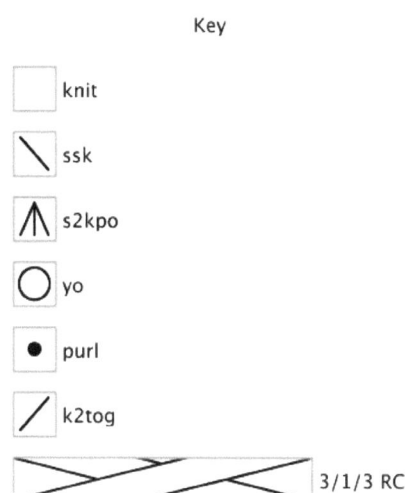

Key

- knit
- ssk (\)
- s2kpo (⋀)
- yo (○)
- purl (●)
- k2tog (/)
- 3/1/3 RC

3/1/3RC: slip 4 stitches to cable needle, hold to back of work, k3, slip centre stitch back to left hand needle and knit it, then k3 from cable needle.

Embleton
Tracey Todhunter

Sometimes it's nice to let the yarn do the talking in a project, and in Embleton the simple design really lends itself to doing just that. This cosy cowl is brilliantly quick, easy and addictive. It is perfect for cooler autumn days and the cold of winter, sitting nicely around the collar and warding off the chilly wind. The design is also easy to play with and modify, with stripes, different sizing, or a ruffled edging.

Materials

Eden Cottage Yarns Whitfell DK (DK, 100% baby Alpaca; 100m / 109yds per 50g ball)
Shade: Natural; 2 x 50g balls

Ruffled version

Shade: Charcoal; 2 x 50g balls
Shade: Laburnum; 1 x 50g ball

Striped version

Shade: Steel; 1 x 50g ball
Shade: Laburnum; 1 x 50g ball
Shade: Natural; 1 x 50g ball
Shade: Misty Woods; 1 x 50g ball
Shade: Charcoal; 1 x 50g ball
Shade: Ebony; 1 x 50g ball

Sample total yarn used approx. 208m (227 yds) as follows:
Steel 78m (85 yds); Laburnum 26m (28 yds); Natural 39m (42.5 yds); Misty Woods 26m (28 yds); Charcoal 26m (28 yds); Ebony 13m (14yds).

Needles and Accessories

4mm crochet hook (or the size needed to obtain the correct gauge)

A locking stitch marker or a safety pin may be used to mark the last dc of each round if required.

Sizes

Finished circumference once blocked: 67cm / 26.5in

Height:
No frill: 18cm / 7in
With optional frill: 21cm / 8.25in

Gauge

15 sts and 14 rnds to 10cm (4in) over half treble pattern using 4mm hook after blocking.
18 sts and 22 rnds to 10cm (4in) over double crochet using 4mm hook after blocking.
Note: Adjust hook size if necessary to match gauge.

Special Techniques

htr: half treble

htr-bar: work half treble into the bar below the stitch on the back of the fabric

htr space: work htr into the space below htr of previous row (ie under all three strands of the stitch)

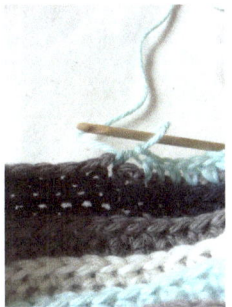

Weave in ends as you go using this helpful tutorial. http://www.cherryheartcrochet.co.uk/2014/09/weaving-in-ends-as-you-go.html

Pattern

Pattern is worked in rounds after the first row.

With 4mm hook and MC make 102 ch.

Rnd 1 (RS): 1 htr into 3rd ch from hk, 1 htr in each ch to end. 100 htr
Join into a rnd by sl st into the top of your ch at the beginning of the row, taking care not to twist the chain.
Rnd 2: 2 ch, 1 htr-bar into each htr to end of row, join with a sl st to top of 2 ch.
Rnd 3: 2 ch, 1 htr space into each htr to end.
Repeat Rnds 2 and 3 a total of 15 times, then work rnd 2 once more.

Fasten off yarn and weave in ends.
Block to measurements.

Ruffled trim: (worked the same for top and bottom)
Ruffled trim is worked in spirals, at end of each rnd, do not turn and do not join with a sl st.

Rnd 1: With MC, join yarn to any htr with a sl st, 1 dc in each dc around, change to CC on last yarn over of last dc, cut MC. 100 dc
Rnd 2: 1 dc in each dc to end.
Rnd 2: 2dc in each dc to end. 200 dc
Rnd 3: 2 dc in each dc to end, sl st into first dc, fasten off yarn and weave in ends. 400 dc

Fasten off yarn and weave in ends.
Block to measurements.

Striped version:

For a striped cowl, work foundation chain and rnds 1-3 in first colour, change to next colour and work rnds 2 and 3. Change colour and work rnds 2 and 3, repeating until there are 15 stripes. Work one more rnd 2 in final colour.

To avoid sewing in many ends after the cowl is finished, work the yarn ends in as you go. To do this, simply hold the previous yarn end alongside the row you are crocheting into, so that the newly created stitches crochet over it.

Fasten off yarn. Block to measurements.

Swale
Karie Westermann

Designed to be the ultimate comfort knit, the Swale hap is knitted almost entirely in soothing garter stitch using two colours of the irresistible Whitfell DK. The simplicity of the design will delight beginner knitters curious about the hap construction; more experienced knitters will love how quickly the pattern works up. The surprisingly simple garter stitch lace edging adds a touch of sophistication to the pattern. This beautiful shawl is a brilliant multi-season knit as well; it's cosy to snuggle around your neck in the winter, and provides a great single layer in place of a cardigan on cool summer evenings.

Materials

Eden Cottage Yarns Whitfell DK (DK; 100% baby Alpaca; 100m / 109yds per 50g ball)
MC shade: Dogwood ; 5 x 50g balls
CC shade: Ebony; 1 x 50g ball

Second sample shown in MC: Laburnum and CC: Charcoal

Needles and Accessories

5mm (US 8) circular needle, 80cm (32in) length (or the size needed to obtain the correct gauge)

Note: the shawl is knitted flat, but circular needles are recommended due to the number of stitches you will be picking up.

One stitch marker (to mark RS)

Sizes

One size
200cm (78.75in) wingspan x 80cm (31.5in) depth

Gauge

15 sts and 20 rows to 10cm (4in) over garter stitch on 5mm needles after blocking.
Note: Adjust needle size if necessary to match gauge.

Pattern Notes

This pattern uses the traditional hap shawl construction. You start by knitting a triangle with loops at the side edges. You then cast off the top of triangle (keeping one stitch on your needle) and pick up the loops from the side edges. The lace edging is knitted on sideways with every last stitch, on the WS, of the edging knitted together with a stitch from the shawl body.

The middle section features an easy stripe pattern. You work four rows in the main colour, then two rows in the contrast colour whilst keeping shaping correct. As you are working in garter stitch, this will look like two garter stitch ridges in the main colour, followed by one ridge in the contrast colour.

Pattern

Triangle Section

Using MC, cast on 1 st.
Row 1: Yo, k 1. 2 sts
Row 2: Yo , k2. 3 sts
Row 3: Yo, k3. 4 sts
Row 4: Yo, k4. 5 sts
Row 5: Yo, k5. 6 sts

Place marker through mid stitch on row 6 to indicate this is RS. You will not be slipping this marker.

Row 6 (RS): *Yo, k to end. 7 sts

Row 6 establishes g st patt with 1 st inc per row worked. Rep row 6 until you have 124 sts and RS facing for next row.

Cast off 123 sts using stretchy cast-off: k2, sl both sts back on LH needle, *k2tog, k1, sl both sts back on LH needle; rep from * until 1 st rem.

Keeping rem st on your RH needle, pick up and knit 61 sts on the LH side of the g st triangle, pm, m1 (at tip of triangle), pm, pick up and knit 62 sts. 125 sts

Next row (WS): K to end.

Middle Section

Using MC

Row 1 (RS): K1, pm, kfb, k to 1 st from marker, kfb, sm, k1, sm, kfb, k to last 2 sts, kfb, pm, k1. 129 sts
Row 2 (WS): Knit.
Row 3 (RS): K1, sm, kfb, k to 1 st from marker, kfb, sm, k1, sm, kfb, k to last 2 sts, kfb, sm, k1. 133 sts
Row 4 (WS): Knit.

Change to CC

Row 5 (RS): K1, pm, kfb, k to 1 st from marker, kfb, sm, k1, sm, kfb, k to last 2 sts, kfb, pm, k1. 137 sts
Row 6 (WS): Knit.
Repeat established six row stripe sequence, six more times. Then work rows 1 and 2 only in MC. 213 sts
Next row (RS): K1, remove marker, kfb, k to 1 st from marker, kfb, remove marker, kfb, remove marker, kfb, k to last 2 sts, kfb, remove marker, k1. 218 sts

Knitted on Lace Edging

Using MC, cast on 10 sts using the cable cast-on technique.

You now have 11 sts on which to work the edging as the first shawl st counts as part of the edging.
Next set-up row: K10 sts, k2tog next st tog with st from shawl body.

Work Edging Chart across all sts 108 times.

After completing all repeats, cast off rem stitches. Soak in lukewarm water and block to measurements.

Written Instructions

Row 1 (RS): Sl1, k2, (yo, ssk, k1) twice, (yo, yo, k1) twice.
Row 2 (WS): K1, (p1, k1) into double-yo, k1, (p1, k1) into double-yo, k8, k2tog.
Row 3 (RS): Sl1, k2, yo, ssk, k1, yo, ssk, k7.
Row 4 (WS): Cast off 4 sts, k10, k2tog.

Chart

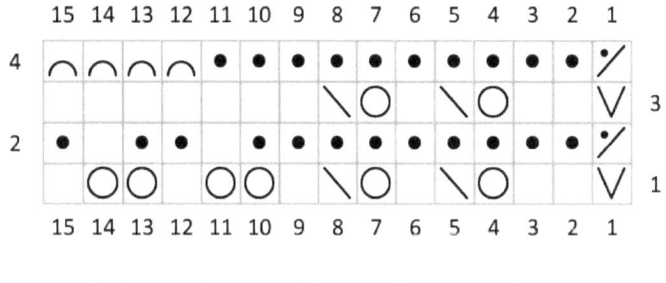

Bothel
Tracey Todhunter

A great all-rounder that you'll reach for time and again on a cold, frosty morning. This beautiful hat is a classic, with subtle stitch patterning that looks complex, yet is easy to execute. The hat works well as either a beanie fit or a slouchy fit, and has an optional bobble or cute loop. Ideal for beginners, it's also a quick, satisfying project for more experienced crocheters.

Materials

Eden Cottage Yarns Whitfell DK (DK; 100% baby Alpaca; 100m / 109yds per 50g ball)
Shade: Laburnum; 2 x 50g balls
Shade: Charcoal; 2 x 50g balls
Shade: Ebony; 2 x 50g balls
Small oddments in contrasting colour for tab top or pom pom if desired.

Small size shown in Ebony
Medium size shown in Laburnum with Charcoal pompom
Large size shown in Charcoal with Laburnum loop top

Needles and Accessories

4.5mm crochet hook (or the size needed to obtain the correct gauge)

A locking stitch marker or a small safety pin may be used to mark the last dc of each round if required.

Sizes

Small (medium, large)
Finished circumference:
50 (52, 56)cm / 19.5 (21,22)in, after blocking
To fit: 50 (55, 60)cm / 20 (22, 24)in
Length: 21(23, 24)cm / 8.5 (9, 9.5)in after blocking

Gauge

First five rounds measure 5cm across the shorter diameter of the hexagon, using 4.5mm hook after blocking.

16 sts and 20 rnds to 10cm (4in) over brim pattern using 4.5mm hook after blocking.

Note: Adjust hook size if necessary to match gauge.

Pattern Notes

The hat is worked in spirals from the centre top; do not turn and do not join at the end of each round unless indicated in pattern.
It is helpful to mark the last stitch of the round with a marker.

Pattern

With 4.5mm hook make 4ch, join with a sl st to make a ring.

Crown increasing:

Rnd 1: 6 dc into ring. 6 dc
Rnd 2: (2 dc in each dc) 6 times. 12 dc
Rnd 3: (1 dc in next dc, 2 dc in next dc) 6 times. 18 dc
Rnd 4: (1 dc in each of next 2 dc, 2 dc in next dc) 6 times. 24 dc
Rnd 5: (1 dc in each of next 3 dc, 2 dc in next dc) 6 times. 30 dc
Rnd 6: (1 dc in each of next 4 dc, 2 dc in next dc) 6 times. 36 dc
Rnd 7 onwards: Continue to increase 6 dc evenly on each round (by working an extra dc before increase) until you have 72 (78, 84 dc).

Hat body (still working in the round, without increasing)
Rnd 13 (14, 15): 1 dc in each dc around. 72 (78, 84) dc
Continue to work 1 dc in each dc around until hat measures 12 (13, 14) cm from the centre/top.

Brim:

(Brim is worked in spirals, do not join and do not turn at the end of each rnd).
Next Rnd: 1 dcblo in each dc to end of rnd. 72 (78, 84) sts
Continue until hat measures 21 (23, 24) cm from rnd 1 (or desired length)

Fasten off yarn and weave in ends.

Block to measurements before adding the optional tab top or pompom.

Tab top: (leave a long tail at beginning and end to sew tab to hat.)
Make 20 ch.

Row 1: 1 sl st in 2nd ch from hk, 1 sl st in each ch to end.

Fold tab in half and sew into a loop. Tie yarn tails together, with a tapestry needle and slip the yarn tails through centre hole of hat. Sew securely into place. Weave in ends.

Pom pom:

Alternatively, you may wish to make a pom pom using a plastic pom pom maker or two cardboard circles of 5cm diameter. Leave a long end to sew neatly to top of hat.

Turbine
Justyna Lorkowska

You'll feel so pretty in this lusciously soft cardigan that you'll want to twirl round and round as its name implies. Reverse stocking stitch showcases the beautiful squishiness of the yarn, while slender fingers of cabled twisted rib make the round yoke especially flattering. Cleverly detailed ribbing at the cuffs and hem, along with a pronounced faux side seam, provide a measure of subtle but classy styling. This incredibly flattering garment is available in seven sizes.

Materials

Eden Cottage Yarns Whitfell DK (DK weight; 100% baby Alpaca; 100m / 109yds per 50g ball)
Shade: Ebony 8 (9, 10, 11, 13, 14, 15) x 50g balls

Needles and Accessories

3.75mm (US 5) circular needle, 80cm (32in) length (or the size needed to obtain the correct gauge)
3.25mm (US 3) circular needle, 80cm (32in) length
One set of 3.75mm (US 5) double-pointed needles (or the size needed to obtain the correct gauge)
One set of 3.25mm (US 3) double-pointed needles

2 cable needles, waste yarn, stitch markers, 10 buttons (about 12mm / 0.75in in diameter), tapestry needle.

Sizes

XS (S, M, L, XL, 2XL, 3XL)
Finished circumference: 82 (91.5, 101, 112.5, 124, 133.5, 141)cm / 32.25 (36, 39.75, 44.25, 48.75, 52.5, 55.5)in
Intended to fit with anywhere from 2.5 cm / 1in negative ease to 2.5 cm / 1in positive ease at bust.

See schematic for detailed measurements.

Gauge

21 sts and 26.5 rows to 10cm (4in) over reverse stocking stitch on 3.75mm (US 5) needles, after blocking.

Note: Adjust needle size if necessary to match gauge.

Pattern Notes

The cardigan is worked from top to bottom. You will cast on stitches for the neck opening and work the Turbine Chart back and forth as you begin increasing. Short rows are worked at the back neckline for proper fit. Increases worked every few rounds create a rounded yoke. Once this shaping is complete, raglan increases are worked down to the underarm.

The cardigan is worked mostly in reverse stocking stitch. After dividing the body from the sleeves, you will shape the body under each arm and work down to the twisted rib hem. The 3/4 sleeves are worked last. They are worked in the round and finished with a twisted rib cuff to match the body.

German Twisted Cast-on: you may refer to http://www.youtube.com/watch?v=BfFadEumBak

Backwards Loop Cast-on Method: *Wrap yarn around left thumb from front to back and secure in palm with other fingers. Insert needle upwards through strand on thumb. Slip loop from thumb onto RH needle, pulling yarn to tighten. Repeat from * for desired number of sts.

Short Rows (wrap-and-turn method):
I recommend visiting:
http://www.knitty.com/ISSUEsummer03/FEATbonnetric.html (scroll down to photo tutorial)

http://www.knittinghelp.com/videos/advanced-techniques (video, scroll down to "Short Row with Wrap")

In order to make the wrapped stitches invisible in reverse stocking stitch, you need to pick up the wrap and place it back on the needle (behind work on RS and on WS) with the stitch you will be working. Work those two stitches together.

1/1/1 LpT: Sl 1 st to cn and hold to front, sl 1 st to 2nd cn and hold to back, k1tbl, p1 from 2nd cn, k1tbl from 1st cn.

Reverse Stocking Stitch (flat)
Row 1 (RS): Purl.
Row 2 (WS): Knit.

Reverse Stocking Stitch (in the round)
Purl every round.

Twisted Rib (flat) – worked over an odd number of sts
Row 1 (RS): k1, *k1tbl, p1; rpt from * to last 2 sts, k1tbl, k1.
Row 2 (WS): p1, *p1tbl, k1; rpt from * to last 2 sts, p1tbl, p1.

Twisted Rib (in the round) - worked over even number of sts
Rnd 1 (RS): *k1tbl, p1; rpt from * to end.

Pattern

Yoke

Using smaller needle and German Twisted Cast-on method, cast on 109 (109, 117, 117, 117, 125, 125) sts.

Set-up row (WS): P1, *p1tbl, k1; rpt from * to last 2 sts, p1tbl, p1.
Work back and forth in twisted rib for 2.5cm / 1in, ending with WS row.
Change to larger needles.

Please refer to chart on page 82

Next row (RS): Begin working Turbine Chart – Row 1.
Work Rows 1-16 of the chart once. 106 (106, 114, 114, 114, 122, 122) sts inc
Total 215 (215, 231, 231, 231, 247, 247) sts.

Next row (RS): Purl.
Short row 1 (WS): K120 (120, 128, 128, 128, 136, 136), w&t.
Short row 2 (RS): P25 (25, 25, 25, 25, 25, 25), w&t.
Short row 3 (WS): K to last wrapped st, pick up the wrap and work it together with the st, k9, w&t.
Short row 4 (RS): P to last wrapped st, pick up the wrap and work it together with the st, p9, w&t.
Rpt Short rows 3 and 4: 3 (3, 3, 3, 4, 4, 4) times more.
Next row (WS): K to end, picking up the last wrap.
Next row (RS): P to end, picking up the last wrap.

Yoke Increases

Work increases as follows for your chosen size:

Size XS
Inc row 1 (RS): P6, (M1Lp, p13) 4 times, (M1Lp, p14) 7 times, (M1Lp, p13) 4 times, (M1Lp, p7). 231 sts.

Size S
Inc row 1 (RS): P2, (M1Lp, p4) 2 times, (M1Lp, p5) 39 times, (M1Lp, p4) 2 times, M1Lp, p2. 259 sts.

Size M
Inc row 1 (RS): P2, (M1Lp, p4) 4 times, (M1Lp, p5) 39 times, (M1Lp, p4) 4 times, M1Lp, p2. 279 sts.

Size L
Inc row 1 (RS): P1, (M1Lp, p3) 20 times, (M1Lp, p4) 27 times, (M1Lp, p3) 20 times, M1Lp, p2. 299 sts.

Size XL
Inc row 1 (RS): P2 (M1Lp, p4) 14 times, (M1Lp, p5) 23 times, (M1Lp, p4) 14 times, M1Lp, p2. 283 sts.
Work 7 rows in reverse stocking st.
Inc Row 2 (RS): P3, (M1Lp, p7) 18 times, (M1Lp, p8) 3 times, (M1Lp, p7) 18 times, M1Lp, p4. 323 sts.

Size 2XL
Inc row 1 (RS): P2, (M1Lp, p4) 6 times, (M1Lp, p5) 39 times, (M1Lp, p4) 6 times, M1Lp, p2. 299 sts.
Work 7 rows in reverse stocking st.
Inc Row 2 (RS): P2, (M1Lp, p5) 6 times, (M1Lp, p6) 39 times, (M1Lp, p5) 6 times, M1Lp, p3. 351 sts.

Size 3XL
Inc row 1 (RS): P2, (M1Lp, p4) 6 times, (M1Lp, p5) 39 times, (M1Lp, p4) 6 times, M1Lp, p2. 299 sts.
Work 7 rows in reverse stocking st.
Inc Row 2 (RS): P2, (M1Lp, p4) 30 times, (M1Lp, p5) 11 times, (M1Lp, p4) 30 times, M1Lp, p2. 371 sts.

All sizes
Work 6 (8, 8, 8, 6, 8, 8) rows in reverse stocking st.

Raglan Shaping

Set-up row (WS): K35 (40, 44, 47, 51, 55, 58), pm, k46 (50, 52, 56, 60, 66, 70), pm, k69 (79, 87, 93, 101, 109, 115), pm, k46 (50, 52, 56, 60, 66, 70), pm, k35 (40, 44, 47, 51, 55, 58).

Row 1 (RS): *P to 1 st before marker, M1Lp, p1, sm, p1, M1Lp; rpt from * 3 times, p to end. 8 sts inc
Row 2 (WS): Knit.

Rpt last two rows 0 (1, 4, 4, 5, 6, 6) times. 71 (83, 97, 103, 113, 123, 129) sts for back; 36 (42, 49, 52, 57, 62, 65) sts for each front; 48 (54, 62, 66, 72, 80, 84) sts for each sleeve; total 239 (275, 319, 339, 371, 407, 427) sts.

Sizes (L, XL, 2XL, 3XL) only:
Work (4, 4, 4, 8) rows in reverse stocking st.

Divide for Body and Sleeves (all sizes)

Next row (RS): *P to marker, remove marker, move sleeve sts to waste yarn, using Backwards Loop Method cast on 6 (5, 3, 6, 7, 7, 8) sts, pm, cast on 6 (5, 3, 6, 7, 7, 8) sts; rpt from * once, p to end. 167 (187, 207, 231, 255, 275, 291) sts.

Next row (WS): K to 1 st before marker, p1tbl (twisted st faux seam), sm, k to marker, sm, p1tbl (twisted st faux seam), k to end.

Next row (RS): P to 1 st before marker, k1tbl (twisted st faux seam), sm, p to marker, sm, k1tbl (twisted st faux seam), p to end.

Work in reverse stocking st with twisted st faux seams for 5cm/2in ending with a WS row.

Waist Shaping

Dec row (RS): P to 3 sts before marker, p2tog, k1tbl, sm, p2tog tbl, p to 2 sts before marker, p2tog, sm, k1tbl, p2tog tbl, p to end. 4 sts dec

Rpt dec row every 10th row 3 times. 151 (171, 191, 215, 239, 259, 275) sts.

Cont in patt with no decs for 7 rows.

Inc row (RS): P to 2 sts before marker, M1Lp, p1, k1tbl, sm, p1, M1Lp, p to 1 st before marker, M1Lp, p1, sm, k1tbl, p1, M1Lp, p to end. 4 sts inc

Rpt inc row every 8th row 3 times. 167 (187, 207, 231, 255, 275, 291) sts.

Cont in patt until garment measures 33cm/13in from underarm or 8cm/3.25in less than your desired length, ending with a WS row.

Next row (RS): P to 2 sts before marker, M1Lp, p1, k1tbl, sm, p to marker, sm, k1tbl, p1, M1Lp, p to end. 169 (189, 209, 233, 257, 277, 293) sts.

Work one WS row in patt removing markers.

Bottom Hem

Change to smaller size needle.
Set-up row (RS): K1, *k1tbl, p1; rpt from * to last 2 sts, k1tbl, k1.
Work 3 rows in twisted rib.

Next row (RS): Work Row 1 of Turbine Chart.
Cont working in twisted rib until ribbing measures 6 cm/2.5in.

Cast off all sts loosely (or with a larger needle) in patt ending at right front.
Do not cut yarn.

Buttonhole Band

Using the same working yarn and needle start at bottom right and pick up and knit an odd number of sts (approx. 3 sts per 4 rows) along the right front to neck edge.

Next row (WS): Knit.
Next row (RS): K1, *k1tbl, p1; rpt from * to last 2 sts, k1tbl, k1.

Work in twisted rib as est until buttonhole band measures 1.25cm/0.5in from pick-up edge, ending with a WS row.
Place 10 stitch markers evenly spaced for buttonholes.

Next row (RS): *Work in patt until 2 sts before marker, k2tog or p2tog, yo, remove marker; rpt from * 9 times, work to end.
Cont working in twisted rib until buttonhole band measures 2.5 cm/1", ending with a WS row.

Cast off all sts loosely (or with a larger needle) in patt on RS.

Button Band

Using smaller needle, start at top left front (RS facing) and pick up and knit the same number of sts as for the buttonhole band.

Next row (WS): Knit.
Next row (RS): K1, *k1tbl, p1; rpt from * to last 2 sts, k1tbl, k1.

Work in twisted rib until button band measures 2.5 cm/1", ending with a WS row.

Cast off all sts loosely (or with a larger needle) in patt on RS.

Sleeves

Note: these instructions are for working sleeves in the round. However, if you would like to avoid purling in every round I recommend making the sleeves flat. In this case cast on one st at each end of the first row then seam the sleeves after finishing. The stitch counts below are for working in the round; add 2 if working flat.

Place the sts of one sleeve on larger DPNs. Attach yarn and pick up and knit 6 (5, 3, 6, 7, 7, 8), pm, pick up and knit 6 (5, 3, 6, 7, 7, 8) sts, work across sleeve sts and join for working in the round. 60 (64, 68, 78, 86, 94, 100] sts.

Work in reverse stocking stitch for 2.5cm / 1in.

Rnd 1: P2, p2tog, p to 4 sts before marker, p2tog tbl, p2. 2 sts dec
Rnds 2-10: Purl.
Rpt last 10 rnds 6 (7, 6, 8, 8, 9, 9) times. 46 (48, 54, 60, 68, 74, 80) sts rem

Work even until sleeve measures about 39 (40, 41, 42, 42, 43, 43) cm / 15.5 (16, 16.25, 16.75, 16.75, 17.25, 17.25)in from underarm or 6 cm/2.5in less than your desired length.

Change to smaller needles and work 4 rnds in twisted rib.
Next rnd: Work Rnd 1 of Turbine Chart.
Cont working in twisted rib until ribbing measures 6 cm/2.5in then cast off all sts loosely (or with a larger needle) in patt.
Repeat instructions for other sleeve.

Finishing

Weave in loose ends using tapestry needle. Block cardigan to dimensions given in schematic making sure to even out the ribbed sections. Sew buttons opposite buttonholes.

Chart

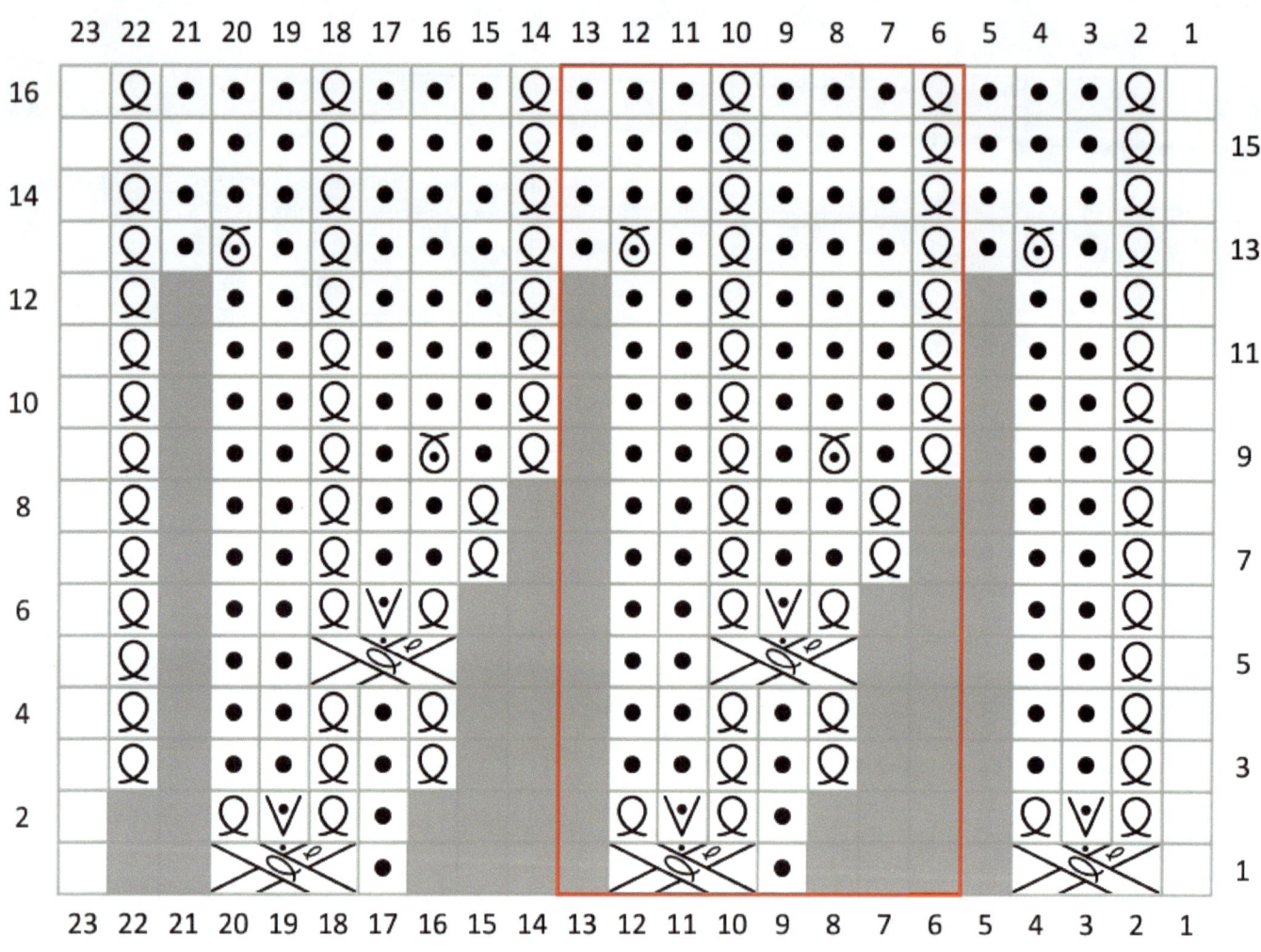

Key

- ☐ RS: knit / WS: purl
- • RS: purl / WS: knit
- Ω RS: k tbl / WS: p tbl
- V WS: kfb
- ⊙ RS: M1Lp
- ▓ grey no stitch
- ▢ One pattern repeat
- ⋈ 1/1/1 LPT

1/1/1 LpT: Sl 1 st to cn and hold to front, sl 1 st to 2nd cn and hold to back, k1tbl, p1 from 2nd cn, k1tbl from 1st cn.

Schematic

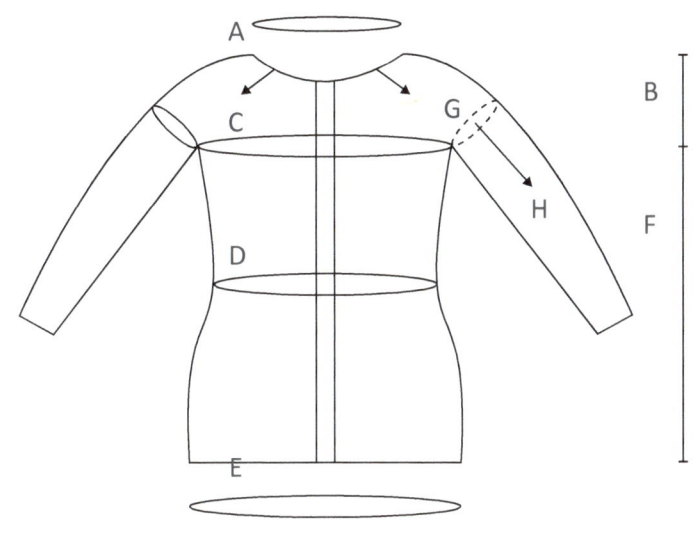

A) Neck opening: 52 (52, 56, 56, 56, 59.5, 59.5) cm / 20.5 (20.5, 22.5, 22.5, 22.5, 23.5, 23.5) in

B) Yoke depth: 14.5 (16, 18.5, 19.5, 23, 25, 26] cm / 5.75 (6.25, 7.25, 7.75, 9, 9.75, 10.25) in

C) Bust: 82 (91.5, 101, 112.5, 124, 133.5, 141) cm / 32.25 (36, 39.75, 44.25, 48.75, 52.5, 55.5) in

D) Waist: 72.5 (82, 95.5, 103, 114.5, 124, 131.5) cm / 28.5 (32.25, 37.5, 40.5, 45, 48.75, 51.75) in

E) Hips: 83 (92.5, 102, 113.5, 125, 134.5, 142) cm / 32.75 (36.5, 40.25, 44.75, 49.25, 53, 56) in

F) Body length from underarm: 39 cm / 15.25 in

G) Sleeve circumference: 28.5 (30.5, 33.5, 37, 41, 45, 47.5) cm / 11.25 (12, 13.25, 14.5, 16.25, 17.75, 18.75) in

H) Sleeve length: 39 (40, 41, 42, 42, 43, 43) cm / 15.5 (16, 16.25, 16.75, 16.75, 17.25, 17.25)in

Button band: 2.5 cm / 1 inch

Calbeck
Tracey Todhunter

Ideal for walking the dog in the woods or to keep your hands warm on days out as the weather turns colder, these quick and easy fingerless mitts are a variation of double crochet, which is good for beginners and more experienced crocheters alike. The larger size can be worn on smaller hands as oversized fingerless mitts, with soft smooshy fabric, or the smaller size can be worn as well-fitting, cosy, warm fingerless mitts. They are easily customisable, by adding ruffles top and bottom, or adding in stripes at any point on the hand.

Materials

Eden Cottage Yarns Whitfell DK (DK; 100% baby Alpaca; 100m / 109yds per 50g ball)

Small sample shown in:
MC Shade: Misty Woods; 2 x 50g balls
CC Shade: Steel; approximately 5g

Larger sample shown in:
Shade: Charcoal; 2 x 50g balls

Sample with ruffles shown in:
MC Shade: Charcoal; 1 x 50g ball
CC Shade: Laburnum; 1 x 50g ball

Needles and Accessories

4.5mm crochet hook (or the size needed to obtain the correct gauge).
A locking stitch marker or a safety pin may be used to mark the last dc of each round if required.

Sizes

Finished circumference: 18 (20)cm / 7 (7.5)in
Length (not including ruffle):
16 (23.5)cm / 6.25 (9.25)in

Gauge

16 sts and 18 rows to 10cm (4in) over cuff pattern using 4.5mm hook after blocking.
18 dc and 20 rows to 10cm (4in) over double crochet using 4.5mm hook after blocking.
Note: Adjust hook size if necessary to match gauge.

Pattern Notes

The cuff is worked in rows, then joined before the hand is worked in spirals.
1 ch at beginning of rows is a turning chain and does not count as a stitch. The larger size is given in brackets.

Pattern

Cuff

With 4.5mm hook and MC make 13 (23) ch fairly loosely.
Row 1: 1 dc into 2nd ch from hk, 1 dc in each ch to end, turn. 12 (22) dc
Row 2: 1 ch, 1 dc in 1st dc, 1 dcblo in each dc to last dc, 1 dc in last dc, turn.
Rows 3 – 29 (33): As Row 2. At the end of last row do not turn.

Joining row - To make the cuff - fold in half with the starting edge furthest from you. Crochet together by working a dc into the back loop of the st of your last row & the whole st of the starting chain row.

Hand

First row: 1 ch, rotate the work 90° so that you will be working into the row ends.
Make 1 dc in last st of each row to end, sl st into first dc to make a ring. 29 (33) dc

The pattern now continues in spirals, at the end of each round, do not turn and do not join with a sl st.
Rnds 1-5: 1 dc in same place as sl st, 1 dc in each dc to end. 29, 33) dc
Rnd 6 (Begin thumb shaping): 13 (15) dc, 2 dc in next dc, 1 dc, 2 dc in next dc, 13 (15) dc. 31 (35) dc
Rnd 7: 13 (15) dc, 2 dc in next dc, 3 dc, 2 dc in next dc, 13 (15) dc. 33 (37) dc
Rnd 8: 13 (15) dc, 2 dc in next dc, 5 dc, 2 dc in next dc, 13 (15) dc. 35 (39) dc
Rnd 9: 13 (15) dc, 2 dc in next dc, 7 dc, 2 dc in next dc, 13 (15) dc. 37 (41) dc
Rnd 10: 13 (15) dc, 2 dc in next dc, 9 dc, 2 dc in next dc, 13 (15) dc. 39 (43) dc

Large size only:
Rnd 11: 15 dc, 2 dc in next dc, 11 dc, 2 dc in next dc, 15 dc. 45 dc

Both sizes:
Rnd 12 (13): 14 (16) dc, miss 11 (13) dc, 1 dc in next dc, 13 (15) dc. 28 (32) dc
Rnd 13 (14) – 19 (20): 1 dc in each dc to end of rnd. (Make any adjustments to length by adding extra rows here).
Rnd 21 (22): 1 sl st in each dc to end of rnd, sl st in first sl st at beg of rnd. Fasten off yarn.

Thumb

Rnd 1: Join yarn to the thumb where it meets the hand, 1 dc in each dc to end. 11 (13) dc
Rnds 2 - 5: 1 dc in each to end.
Rnd 6: 1 sl st in each dc to end. Join to first sl st.
Fasten off yarn, sew side seam. Weave in ends.

Frilled Trim

Frilled trim is worked in spirals - at end of each rnd, do not turn and do not join with a sl st.
Working into the row ends at the bottom of the cuff -
Rnd 1: With MC, join yarn with a sl st to any st along the row end. Work 1 rnd of 1 dc in each row end around, change to CC on last yarn over of last dc, cut MC. 28 (32) sts
Rnd 2: 1 dc in each dc to end.
Rnd 2: 2 dc in each dc to end. 56 (64) dc
Rnd 3: 2 dc in each dc to end, sl st into first dc 112 (118) dc
Fasten off yarn and weave in ends.

Alternatively, work last two rounds of hand and thumb in a contrasting colour.

Variations to Pattern

The cuff can easily be made longer or shorter to suit the wearer. For a looser fit, the slip stitch rounds can be omitted.
Block lightly before wearing.

Honey Bee
Dani Sunshine

A classic children's sweater with gorgeous detailing. Worked from the top down, this easy pattern is the perfect knit for the little ones in your life. Buttery soft Whitfell DK will keep them warm and cozy whilst they do what they do best: playing hard. This versatile design is simple and stylish; the perfect utility piece for adventurous kids. Available in six sizes from 3 months to 10 years.

Materials

Eden Cottage Yarns Whitfell DK (DK; 100% baby Alpaca; 100m / 109yds per 50g ball)
Shade: Dogwood; 3 (3, 4, 4, 5, 6, 7) x 50g balls

Needles and Accessories

4mm (US 6) circular needle, 40 (40, 60, 60, 60, 60, 60) cm / 16 (16, 24, 24, 24, 24, 24)in length (or the size needed to obtain the correct gauge)
3.5mm (US4) circular needle, 40 (40, 60, 60, 60, 60, 60)cm / 16 (16, 24, 24, 24, 24, 24)in length (or the size needed to obtain the correct gauge)

One set of 4mm / US6 double pointed needles, for sleeves
One set of 3.5mm / US4 double pointed needles, for cuffs

Note: you can use the magic loop method with an 80cm / 32in circular for both body and sleeves, thereby omitting the need for DPNs.

8 stitch marker, holders / waste yarn, tapestry needle, 2 (2, 2, 3, 3, 3, 3) small buttons

Sizes

3-6 m (6-12m, 1-2y, 3-4y, 5-6y, 7-8y, 9-10y)

To fit chest size: 43 (47, 51, 56, 61, 66, 71)cm / 17 (18.5, 20, 22, 24, 26, 28)in
with approx. 5cm / 2in of positive ease
Actual chest circumference: 50 (53, 59, 62, 68, 71, 77) cm / 20 (21.5, 23.5, 25, 27, 28.5, 30.75)in

Gauge

22 sts and 28 rows to 10cm (4in) over stocking stitch, in the round on 4mm needles after blocking.

Note: Adjust needle size if necessary to match gauge.

Pattern Notes

This sweater is worked seamlessly from the top down. The yoke is worked back and forth with raglan increases. The fronts are then joined and the sleeves and body are worked in the round. Hems and neckline are finished with garter stitch.

Backwards loop cast on:
Holding the working yarn in your left hand, move your left thumb behind and under the yarn so the yarn makes a loop around your thumb. Insert the RH needle through the loop from the front, pull tight.

Garter Stitch
Flat: Knit all rows.
In the round: Knit 1 rnd, purl one rnd to make one garter ridge.

Pattern

With larger needles, CO 36 (38, 40, 40, 46, 48, 50) sts.

Set up Row (WS):
P1, pm, p1, pm, p4 (4, 4, 4, 6, 6, 6), pm, p1, pm, p22 (24, 26, 26, 28, 30, 32) pm, p1, pm, p4 (4, 4, 4, 6, 6, 6), pm, p1, pm, p1.

Raglan increases:
Row 1 (RS): K to marker, M1R, sm, k1, sm, M1L, k to marker, M1R, sm, k1, sm, M1L, k to marker, M1R, sm, k1, sm M1L, k to marker, M1R, sm, k1, sm, M1L, k to end. 44 (46, 48, 48, 54, 56, 58) sts
Row 2 (WS): Purl.
Work these two rows 3 (3, 4, 4, 5, 5, 6) more times. 68 (70, 80, 80, 94, 96, 106) sts
Cut yarn.

With RS facing and using backwards loop method, CO sts for the fronts to the beginning and end of each row as follows:
CO 9 (10, 11, 11, 12, 13, 14) sts to RH needle, continue with working yarn following RS increase row 1 as above, CO 9 (10, 11, 11, 12, 13, 14) sts.
Next row (WS): Purl.
94 (98, 110, 110, 126, 130, 142) sts

Honey Bee Pattern

You will now continue with raglan increases while working the Honey Bee pattern on the right and left fronts. Please refer to the charts and written instructions on pages 89 and 90.

Row 3 (RS): Work Honey Bee Left Front to marker, M1R, sm, k1, sm, M1L, k to marker, M1R, sm, k1, sm, M1L, k to marker, M1R, sm, k1, sm M1L, k to marker, M1R, sm, k1, M1L, work Honey Bee Right Front to end of row. 102 (106, 118, 118, 134, 138, 150) sts
Row 4 (WS): Purl.

Work these two rows 7 (8, 8, 10, 11, 12, 13) more times.
158 (170, 182, 198, 222, 234, 254) sts

Work row 1 (increase row) once more.
166 (178, 190, 206, 230, 242, 262) sts

Cut yarn.

Join for working in the round and move the beginning of the round to the underarm as follows:

With RS facing, slip the 24 (26, 28, 30, 33, 35, 38) left front sts onto RH needle, remove marker, slip1, place BOR marker, k32 (34, 36, 40, 46, 48, 52) sleeve sts, sm, k1, remove marker, k50 (54, 58, 62, 68, 72, 78) back sts, remove marker, k1, sm, k32 (34, 36, 40, 46, 48, 52) sleeve sts, sm, k1, remove marker, k24 (26, 28, 30, 33, 35, 38) right front sts, CO 3 sts using backwards loop CO, k25 (27, 29, 31, 34, 36, 39) remaining left front sts. This is the new beginning of the round.

Separate body and sleeves:

Slip BOR marker, place the next 32 (34, 36, 40, 46, 48, 52) sts on a holder for the 1st sleeve, remove marker, CO 2 (2, 4, 4, 4, 4, 4) sts using backwards loop CO, k to marker, remove marker, place the next 32 (34, 36, 40, 46, 48, 52) sts on a holder for the 2nd sleeve, remove marker, CO 2 (2, 4, 4, 4, 4, 4) sts, k to end of round.
There are 109 (117, 129, 137, 149, 157, 169) sts for the body and 32 (34, 36, 40, 46, 48, 52) sts for each sleeve.

Work on body sts in the round:

Work in st st in the round until piece measures 15 (15, 20, 25, 28, 30, 33)cm / 6 (6, 8, 10, 11, 12, 13)in from the underarm, or until approx. 2.5 cm/ 1in less than desired length.

Work one decrease round as follows:
*Knit 8, k2tog, rep from * until 9 (7, 9, 7, 9, 7, 9) sts remain, k to last 2 sts, k2tog.
98 (105, 116, 123, 134, 141, 152) sts

Beginning with a purl round, work in garter stitch for 5 rounds (makes 3 garter ridges).
BO all sts knitwise.

Sleeves:

Place the 32 (34, 36, 40, 46, 48, 52) sleeve sts onto long circular needle or DPNs.

Starting at centre of the underarm, pick up and knit 1 (1, 2, 2, 2, 2, 2) sts, k all sleeve sts, pick up and knit 1 (1, 2, 2, 2, 2, 2) sts, place marker (if needed) to indicate the beginning of the round.
There are 34 (36, 40, 44, 50, 52, 56) sleeve sts.
Work in st st in the round until sleeve measures 11 (13, 15, 18, 19, 20, 23) cm / 4.5 (5, 6, 7, 7.5, 8, 9)in from the underarm.
Next rnd: k3, k2tog, repeat from * until 4 (6, 5, 4, 5, 7, 6) sts remain, knit to last 2 sts, k2tog.
27 (29, 32, 35, 40, 42, 45) sts

Beginning with a purl round, work in garter stitch for 5 rounds (makes 3 garter ridges).
Cast off all sts knitwise.

Neckline:

With RS facing and using smaller needle, starting at the right front, pick up and knit 1 st for every st along the horizontal edge, of the cable panel, 1 st for every 2 rows along the diagonal edge, 3 sts for every 4 rows along the vertical edge, of the sleeves. Pick up and knit 1 st for every st along the horizontal edge of the shoulders and back. Pick up and knit the same number of sts for the left front as you have for the right. Turn work.

Beginning with a WS row, work 3 rows in garter st. The last row is a WS row.
BO off all sts knitwise on the RS.

Button bands:

Left front:
With RS facing, starting at the top edge of the left front, pick up and knit 15 (17, 17, 20, 21, 22, 24) sts evenly along the vertical edge.
Work 4 rows in garter st.
Cast off all sts knitwise on the WS.

Right front:
With RS facing, pick up and knit 15 (17, 17, 20, 21, 22, 24) sts evenly along the right front.
Row 1 (WS): Knit.

Sizes 3-6m (6-12m, 1-2 y)
Row 2 (RS): Knit 5 (6, 6), yo, k2tog, k5 (6, 6), yo, k2tog, k1.

Sizes 3-4y (5-6y, 7-8y, 9-10y)
Row 2 (RS): Knit 3 (4, 3, 3), yo, k2tog, k5 (5, 6, 7) yo, k2tog, k5 (5, 6, 7), yo, k2tog, k1.

Rows 3 and 4: Knit.

Cast off all sts knitwise on the WS.

Wet block the sweater. Pin the fronts into place for best results.

Key

☐ knit

▨ grey no stitch

⧖ 1/2 RC

⧗ 1/2 LC

1/2 RC: slip 2 sts to cable needle and hold in back, k1, then k2 from cable needle

1/2 LC: slip 1 sts to cable needle and hold in front, k2, then k1 from cable needle

Chart

Note that only RS rows are charted, all WS rows are purled as per instructions on page 87.

3 - 6m Left Front

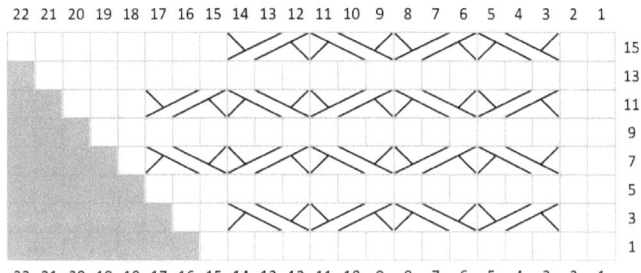

3 - 6m Right Front

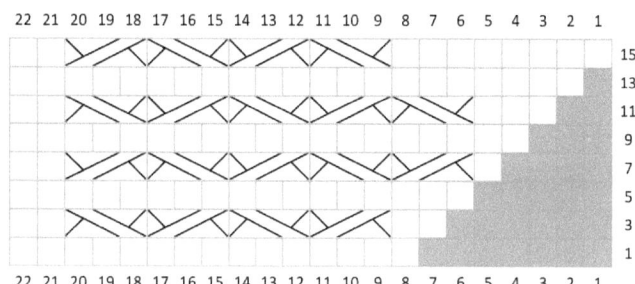

6 - 12m Left Front

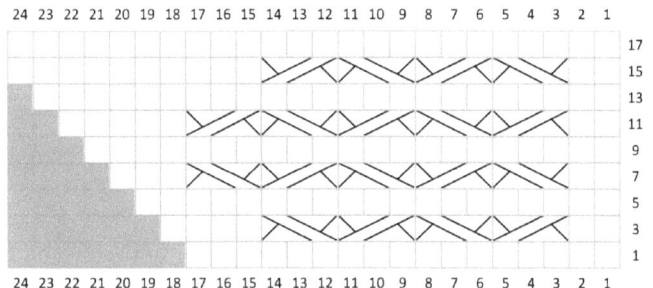

6 - 12m Right Front

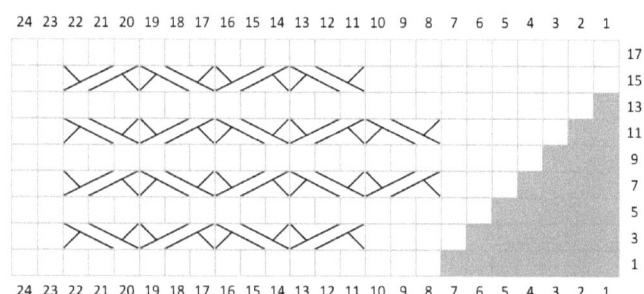

1 - 2y Left Front

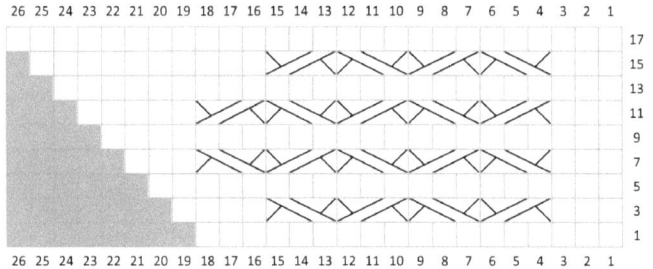

1 - 2y Right Front

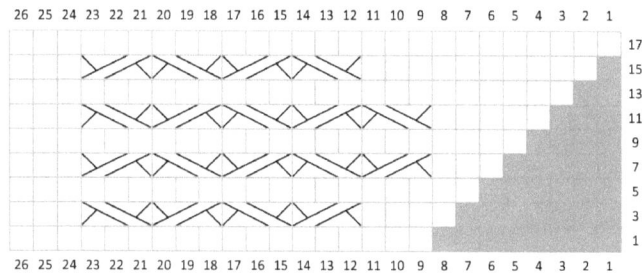

3 - 4y Left Front

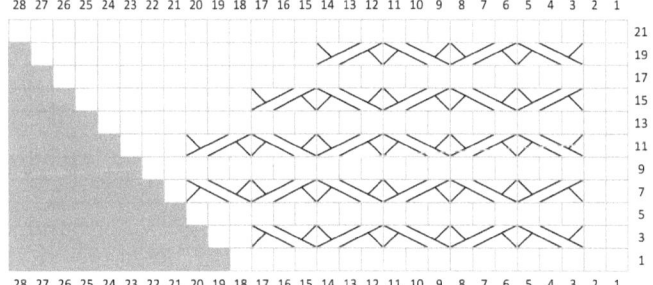

3 - 4y Right Front

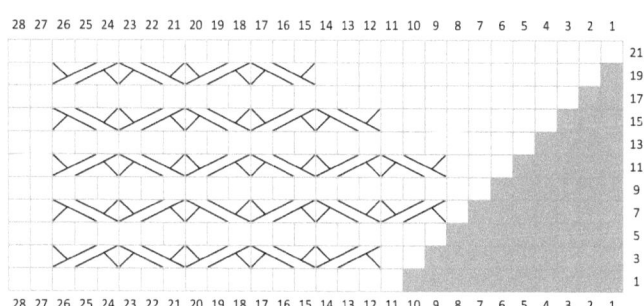

5 - 6y Left Front

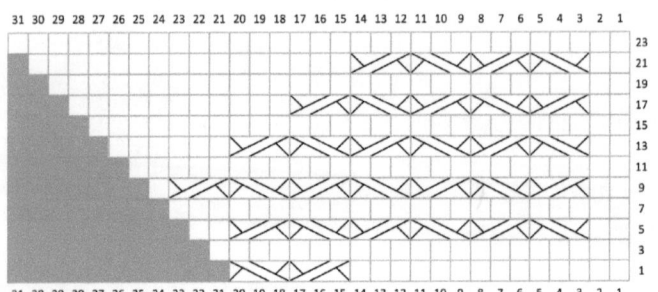

5 - 6y Right Front

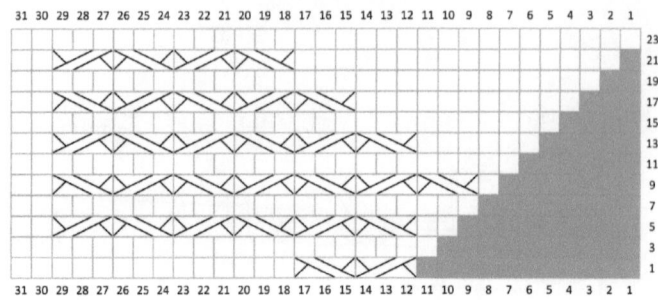

7 - 8y Left Front

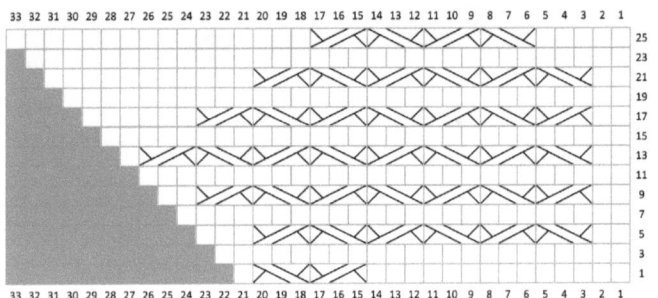

7- 8y Right Front

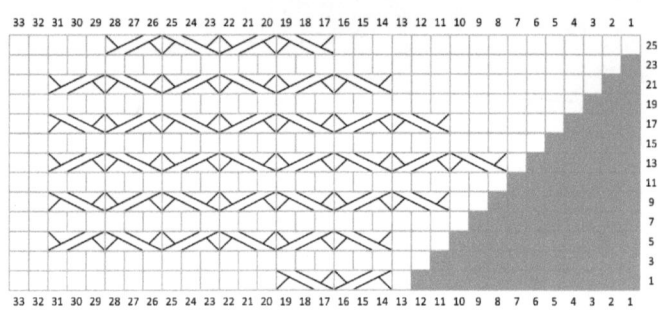

9 - 10y Left Front

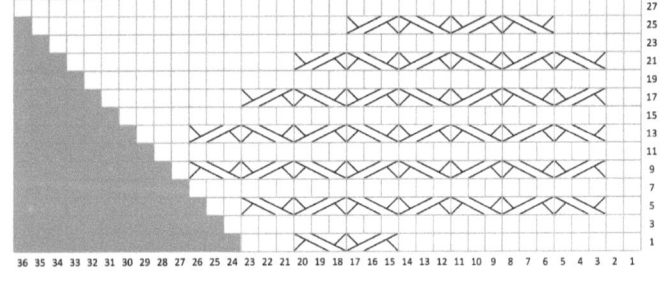

9 - 10y Right Front

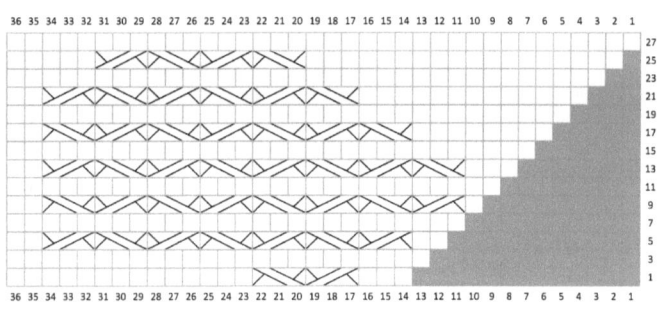

Schematic

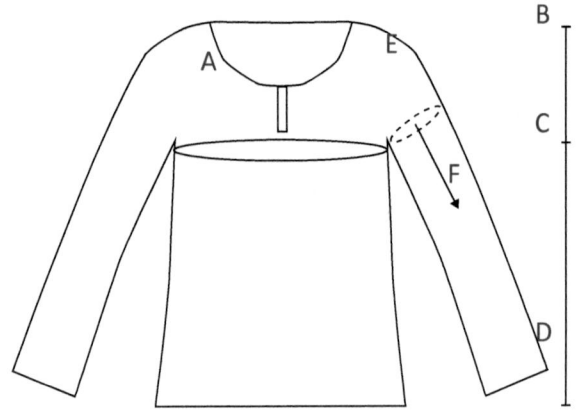

A) Chest circumference: 50 (53, 59, 62, 68, 71, 77)cm / 20 (21.5, 23.5, 25, 27, 28.5, 30.75)in

B) Armhole depth: 12.5 (13, 14, 15.5, 18, 19, 20.5)cm/ 5 (5.25, 5.5, 6.25, 7, 7.5, 8)in

C) Length from underarm: 17.5 (17.5, 22.5, 27.5, 30.5, 32.5, 35.5)cm / 7 (7, 9, 11, 12, 13, 14)in

D) Full length: 30 (30.5, 36.5, 43, 48.5, 51.5, 56)cm / 12 (12.25, 14.5, 17.25, 19, 20.5, 22)in

E) Sleeve circumference: 15.5 (16.5, 18, 20, 23, 23.5, 25.5)cm / 6 (6.5, 7, 7.75, 9, 9.25, 10)in

F) Sleeve length: 11 (13, 15, 18, 19, 20, 23)cm / 4.5 (5, 6, 7, 7.5, 8, 9)in

Abbreviations

1/1/1 LpT	Sl 1 st to cn and hold to front, sl 1 st to 2nd cn and hold to back, k1tbl, p1 from 2nd cn, k1tbl from 1st cn.
1/1LC	(left twist) slip 1 st to cable needle and hold in front, k1, then k1 from cable needle
1/1RC	(right twist) slip 1 st to cable needle and hold in back, k1, then k1 from cable needle
1/2LC	slip 1 sts to cable needle and hold in front, k2, then k1 from cable needle
1/2RC	slip 2 sts to cable needle and hold in back, k1, then k2 from cable needle
2/1/2 LC	Sl 3st to cn and hold at front. k2 from LH needle. Sl p st from cn back to LH needle and purl it, k2 from cn.
2/1/2 RC	Sl 3st to cn and hold at back. k2 from LH needle. Sl p st from cn back to LH needle and purl it, k2 from cn.
3/1/3RC	slip 4 stitches to cable needle, hold to back of work, k3, slip centre stitch back to left hand needle and knit it, then k3 from cable needle.
2 dc	work 2 double crochet in same stitch (an increase of one stitch)
alt	alternate
beg	beginning
BO	pass stitch over as if to cast off / bind off
BOR	beginning of round
CC	contrast colour
ch	chain
cn	cable needle
CO	cast on
cont	continue
dc	double crochet
dcblo	double crochet through back loop only
dec	decrease/decreasing
dk	double knit
DPN	double-pointed needle
est	established
foll	following
g st	garter stitch (knit every row)
hk	hook
htr	half treble
htr space	work htr into the space below htr of previous row (ie. under all three strands of the stitch)
htr-bar	work half treble into the bar below the stitch on the back of the fabric
in	inch(es)
inc	increase/increasing
k	knit
K^	knit through both legs of 'pulled-tight' st (short-row-slipped-st) as if it were a normal, single st
k2tog	knit two stitches together
kfb	knit into front and back of same stitch
kfbf	knit into front, back and front again of same stitch
ktbl	knit through the back loop
LH	left hand
Loop	pull out the cable to loop between the stitches
m	marker
M(x)	marker (x, denotes which marker)

m1	make 1 (as M1L)
M1L(p)	make 1 (left leaning). Bring the tip of the left-hand needle under the strand between stitches, from front to back. Knit (purl) through the back of this loop.
M1R(p)	make 1 (right leaning). Bring the tip of the left-hand needle under the strand between stitches, from back to front. Knit (purl) this loop.
MC	main colour
mm	millimetre(s)
p	purl
P^	purl through both legs of 'pulled-tight' st (short-row-slipped-st) as if it were a normal, single st
p2tog	purl two stitches together
p3tog	purl three stitches together
patt	pattern
pfb	purl into the front and back of the same stitch
pm	place marker
prev	previous
pwise	purlwise
rem	remain/remaining
RH	right hand
rm	remove marker
rnd(s)	round(s)
rpt(s)	repeat(s)
RS	right side
sk2po	slip two stitches together as if to knit, k1, then pass the slipped stitches over. 2 sts dec
Slk2togp	slip 1, knit 2 together, pass slipped stitch over. 2 sts dec
Sl 1	slip one stitch purlwise (unless otherwise directed)
Sl 1^	wyif, sl 1 purlwise, pull on yarn over and behind needle until both legs of st show
sl st	slip stitch
sm	slip marker
ssk	slip two stitches one at a time as if to knit onto the RH needle, insert tip of LH needle into front of two stitches and knit the two stitches together
ssp	slip two stitches knitwise one at a time, purl two slipped stitches together through the back of the loops
st st	stocking stitch
st(s)	stitch(es)
tbl	through the back of the loop
tog	together
w&t	wrap & turn. Take yarn to opposite side of work (between the needles), slip next stitch purlwise from left-hand to right-hand needle, return yarn to original side of work, return slipped stitch to left-hand needle without twisting. The stitch is now wrapped with yarn. Turn work and start next row leaving any remaining stitches unworked.
WS	wrong side
wyib	with yarn behind
wyif	with yarn in front
yfwd	yarn forward
yo	yarn over

On Location

Before we delve in, a word about the magical locations we visited for the photo shoots. You will undoubtedly notice that more of our photographs focus on details within landscapes, rather than landscapes as a whole. Within a large landscape, I am always drawn to the details. Whenever we go out on a photo shoot it takes us ages, as (despite my better intentions) I stop every couple of paces to inspect and photograph little things - colour, form, texture, wildlife, and often, silhouettes.

I've always been fascinated with nature's eye for detail and love using photography to capture it, carefully framing images to share the details that resonate with me.

We hope you love seeing the beautiful places surrounding us that we have used as a backdrop to this collection. I also hope you enjoy journeying with me, catching glimpses of details that captured my imagination in these stunning landscapes.

If you are looking for a great day out, we heartily recommend visits to all of these locations.

The Chevin
(Pimms Cup and Cloudburst)

For Pimms Cup we chose to go to the summit of The Chevin, which is a stretch of woodland and heathland along the ridge and hillside overlooking Otley in West Yorkshire. We are incredibly lucky to have this space (as well as our other locations) so close to ECY headquarters, and the windswept hilltop with views over Yorkshire was the first place that struck me for photographing this hat.

The Chevin has a good variety of woodland, grasses, meadows and heathland. The surrounding areas of farmland are all fenced, off making The Chevin a brilliant spot for dogwalking. It also overlooks the market town of Otley, which is well known for its street markets and great pubs. For those interested in snippets of history, there was a Roman road along The Chevin; part of the link between York, Tadcaster and Ilkley. The name Chevin comes from the British Celtic language word cefyn, cefn, or cefu, which means 'ridge' (of high land).

We also chose The Chevin for Cloudburst, although instead of heading for the summit, we visited the ancient woodland that backs onto beautiful grassland filled with wild flowers. At the right time of day the light in this area is simply magical. We spent some time soaking up the atmosphere and waiting for the perfect moment to photograph the delicate Misty Woods colourway; leaving me plenty of time to capture the delicate beauty of wild grasses and flowers blowing in the wind.

Hardcastle Woods (and Gibson Mill)

Location for Hardcastle and Deco Swirl.

Hardcastle crags and woods is a valley just along from Hebden Bridge in the South Pennines, with the nineteenth century Gibson Mill at the heart of it. The mill itself is an old cotton mill, which is off-grid and run by The National Trust. We sadly didn't have time to look around the inside, but instead spent our time outside exploring the woodland.

The valley is quite small but steep, with a gently bubbling river flowing along the bottom. The space is very enclosed and beautifully lush with foliage everywhere. The walk along the riverside feels like you are entering a sort of wonderland. The light dapples through the trees above, bathing the delicate flowers along the riverside in a soft, golden light; perfect for photography and losing myself in the magical details of this enchanted place.

The mill is further into the valley, a short walk from the carpark, along that wonderful river. Although we didn't have time to fully appreciate the mill, the area is a brilliant day out and much recommended. There is a cafe in the mill for a pit stop (and maybe a spot of knitting with some tea and cake). The whole area covers about 400 acres, perfect for exploring.

More info: http://www.nationaltrust.org.uk/hardcastle-crags/

Yorkshire Dales

Location for Swale and Bothel in Laburnum and Ebony.

This photoshoot was fun. We drove into the Yorkshire Dales and explored a bit. The two shawls are quite different and I wanted to convey the wonderful versatility of this design in the photos. I was impressed at how adaptable the fabric of this shawl is. It can be worn in a really cosy, wintry style, snuggled around the neck, but the shawl also works well as a single layer about the shoulders, creating a lightweight warmth ideal for a cool summer evening, or whilst out and about during the in-between months of spring and autumn.

Our location near Bolton Abbey was wonderfully varied, providing space for us to experiment with both shawls until we settled on lighting we were happy with. The darker colours of the red shawl glowed amongst the riverside woodland, and the soft, light shade of the yellow shawl called out to be photographed amongst the wildflowers and grasses that run along the riverside.

Bothel showcases the subtle sheen and halo of the yarn beautifully. I felt that the simplicity of the riverside grassland, along with the soft colours and lighting, was an ideal setting to highlight the beautiful textures of each stitch.

Although we didn't use Bolton Abbey itself as a location (mostly because, being a Saturday, it was busy), it is a great day out. The area of the Abbey estate is large and provides plenty of space for walking and exploring. There are excellent tearooms and a pub for meals and drinks.

About five miles away, there is also a Billy Bob's 50s style diner which is situated on a working farm. We definitely recommend paying a visit if you are in the area.
For more information on Bolton Abbey: http://www.boltonabbey.com/
For more information on Billy Bob's: http://www.billybobsparlour.com/

Stainburn Forest

Location for Turbine, Bothel (in Charcoal) and Caldbeck.

Stainburn Forest is a Forestry Commission site, located on the edge of the Yorkshire Dales between Otley and Harrogate (and pleasingly, not too far from Blubberhouses, Kettlesing, and Timble).

It is a wonderful location for forest walks. The elevated location offers great glimpses of the landscape beyond. The edge is woodland, with grasses and gnarled trees, however further in it becomes more enclosed and coniferous, with a strangely beautiful ethereal light.

This seemed like an ideal location for Turbine, with its gnarled and twisting cables. The striking details of this gorgeous cardigan were echoed in the natural beauty surrounding us.

The Caldbeck Mitts are great for adding a touch of soft cosy warmth to keep the chill off your hands while exploring. I couldn't resist pulling them on as I explored this woodland wonderland. I was in my element, catching glimpses of the details in trees and along the carpet of pine needles on the woodland floor; a simply magical and enchanting space.

More information: http://www.forestry.gov.uk/stainburnforest
http://www.visitharrogate.co.uk/things-to-do/stainburn-forest-mtb-trails-and-walks-p1221291

The Designers

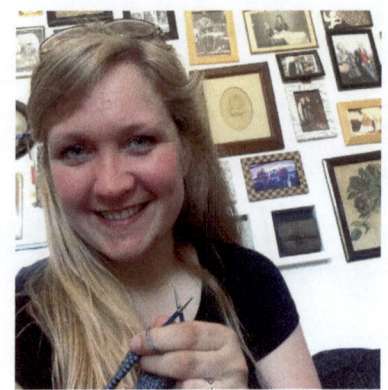

Dieuwke van Mulligen

Dieuwke van Mulligen began knitting at a young age, learning the magic her grandmother worked every time she created a garment for one of her children or grandchildren. Since childhood, she kept the knitting close to heart, picking it up at regular intervals. She loves trying out new constructions and techniques, which often results in new design inspiration. Her main focus is on functional wardrobe additions that she would use herself, generating a wide range of women's garments and accessories. www.knitterskitchen.com

Thea Colman

After many years in advertising, Thea decided to combine her love of knitting and cocktails in a second career. Working with a mix of styles and construction methods in her designs, she loves to find motifs that look more difficult than they actually are. Her patterns often feature a modern twist on a classic or vintage silhouette, and are known for attention to individual fit and often contain descriptive notes in the instructions, so knitters can adapt each garment to best suit their figure. Each pattern is named after a cocktail, the recipes for which are always posted on her blog. www.babycocktails.com

Louise Tilbrook

Louise Tilbrook is an enthusiastic (some would say obsessed) sock knitter. Taught to knit at a young age, she encountered Ravelry and hasn't looked back since. A northern girl at heart, she is inspired by frequent visits to the beautiful English Lake District and loves cables, simple, stylish lace and soft subtle colours of nature. Louise loves to create sock designs that have unisex appeal. www.louisetilbrookdesigns.blogspot.co.uk

Louise Zass-Bangham

Louise Zass-Bangham is the designer behind Inspiration Knits. With a penchant for beautiful, hand painted yarns, Louise delights in designing accessories that will showcase these. Her designs capture simple elements of texture or geometric patterns and combines them with the yarn to create striking accessories which will add excitement to any outfit. Keen to make knitting accessible, she believes patterns should be clearly written and fun to knit. *www.inspirationknits.com*

Åsa Tricosa (Åsa Söderman)

Åsa's style leans towards seamless and clever. This is what inspires her signature top-down Ziggurat technique where everything from cast on to cast off is knitted in one big zig-zaggy sweep from beginning to end — tailored shoulders, set-in sleeves, built-in buttonbands, pockets, and built-in whatever else might be needed. Born and raised in Sweden, she has now knitted her way to Germany where she lives with her Danish husband. Fortunately (for her) the language of knitting is international. *www.asatricosa.com*

Clare Devine

Clare Devine is a writer and designer. Originally from South Africa, she has nomadic tendencies and is currently knitting her way around the UK. She is passionate about all things fibre related (especially if it's grey), knitting, travel and sunshine in equal measures. A natural teacher at heart, she loves creating designs that encourage and inspire knitters to try new skills and techniques. *www.yarnandpointysticks.com*

Tracey Todhunter

Tracey Todhunter is a knitwear designer specialising in crochet homeware and accessories. Regularly featured in many UK craft magazines, she creates designs which are stylish and versatile, with plenty of options to customise to personal taste. A published author, her next book (an encyclopedia of crochet) is due for publication in January 2016. www.grannycoolcrochet.com

Karie Westermann

Karie Westermann was born in Denmark and now lives in Glasgow, Scotland. She works as a knitwear designer and also writes about, translates, and teaches knitting. Her work draws strongly upon her Nordic roots and combines the practices of craft and storytelling. In her spare time, Karie travels around on her red bike, enjoys pub quizzes, and has a lot of opinions about Eurovision. www.kariebookish.net

Justyna Lorkowska

Justyna is a former teacher and a knitwear fanatic. She learned her first stitches from her mom when she was a teenager, but she gave up knitting quickly afterwards. Having her first baby brought back her passion with great impact and this time she also started designing knitwear for adults and children. She lives in Poland and designs knitwear that she would gladly find in her closet: flattering, versatile and seamless. www.letesknits.com

Dani Sunshine

Dani Sunshine is a designer and hand dyer, living on the South Coast of England. Specialising in beautiful semi-solid shades as a dyer, when designing Dani loves to create simple, understated patterns that showcase the yarns to their best effect. She creates wearable, stylish pieces for the whole family to enjoy. www.ravelry.com/designers/dani-sunshine

About Victoria Magnus

Victoria Magnus is an independent hand dyer, knitwear designer and owner of Eden Cottage Yarns. Based in Yorkshire, Victoria is inspired by nature and her surroundings and hand dyes all her yarns in her home kitchen. Every aspect of the operation takes place here, from preparation to finishing and labeling of skeins, ready to grace your needles. Passionate about simplicity and wearability in her designs, Victoria loves to create garments and accessories that are versatile enough to use every day.

Stocked worldwide, Eden Cottage Yarns specialises in high quality natural fibres, dyed to a relaxing and understated palette, to allow the beauty to shine through in your projects.

The Yarn

About the Yarn

Whitfell DK is a classic and versatile yarn, which works well with a wide variety of projects. The 100% baby Alpaca is buttery soft, with a gentle and subtle halo and exquisitely delicate sheen. The fibre is worsted spun giving it a wonderful smooth handle and a beautiful drape.

This versatile yarn can look delicate and smooth, or quite cosy and rustic, depending on the type of project you knit with it. Ultimately, we find it an absolute joy to work with and hope you do too.

Whitfell DK is available in nine gorgeous shades and comes in 50g balls with 100m/109yds per ball.

The Colourways

Eden Cottage Yarns is proud to present our signature Whitfell DK colourways.

Charcoal	Rich, dark, neutral
Dogwood	Bold autumnal burnt red
Ebony	Rich chocolate brown
Fuchsia	Bright, cool pink
Laburnum	Sophisticated, laid-back yellow
Lichen	Fresh zesty green
Misty Woods	Delicate ethereal green
Natural	Complements everything neutral
Steel	The perfect grey!

The Colourways

Yarns, pattern books and much more available on the website
http://www.edencottageyarns.co.uk

Digital patterns available from Ravelry
http://www.ravelry.com/patterns/sources/eden-cottage-yarns

Join in the chatter on the Ravelry Group
http://www.ravelry.com/groups/eden-cottage

Find us on social media
Twitter: @edencottage
Instagram: EdenCottageYarns
Facebook: https://www.facebook.com/pages/Eden-Cottage-Yarns/151573411577273

Email: edencottageyarns@gmail.com

www.ingramcontent.com/pod-product-compliance
Lightning Source LLC
Chambersburg PA
CBHW041441010526
44118CB00003B/142